THE MAN PERFECTLY FILLED WITH THE SPIRIT

The Man perfectly filled with the Spirit

by

John Larsson

International Headquarters of The Salvation Army
101 Queen Victoria Street, London EC4P 4EP

First published 1986
ISBN 085412 497 7

COLONEL JOHN LARSSON, BD (Lond)
became a Salvation Army officer in 1957. He has served in the British, Scotland and South America West Territories, and is currently Training Principal at the William Booth Memorial (International) Training College, London. The colonel is a well-known composer of Army music and the author of *Doctrine Without Tears* and *Spiritual Breakthrough.*

Cover design by Jim Moss

Printed in Great Britain by
The Campfield Press, St Albans

Contents

All Scripture references are from the *New English Bible* unless otherwise stated.

Introduction

THIS is a book for those who yearn to be more like their Lord and Master Jesus Christ. It is for those who feel dissatisfied with themselves as they are and who want to know how their lives might reflect more of the radiant nature and spiritual effectiveness of the Man from Nazareth.

Of course, Jesus was unique. He was the Son of God. But he was not so wholly different that any attempt to be like him need be doomed. For he was also a true human being. He was one of us—a point to which Christian teaching has tenaciously clung. Human nature is something that we share with Jesus.

But we share more. We share an experience of the Holy Spirit. The Spirit that indwelt him indwells us. And if we think of Jesus as *the Man perfectly filled with the Spirit* and ourselves as learners who are but imperfectly filled, new insights open up. And our Lord's experience of that Spirit becomes of vital interest to us, for what he experienced in divine fullness we too in an imperfect and finite way may also experience.

So this is a book about Jesus, about the true beauty of humanity as seen in him. But it is also a book about ourselves, with our inadequacies and longings and strivings for the mind of Christ to become ours. And it is a book about the Holy Spirit, for it is through his work that the Christlike image within us will be brought to completion.

1

Jesus—truly and properly man

THE chorus had been sung a number of times at the close of the musical and the audience was beginning to drift away in a thoughtful mood. The young man looked despondent.

'To be like Jesus—this hope possesses me,' he kept repeating to himself. We sat down to talk.

'That's exactly what I want,' he continued, 'what I feel Christianity is all about—to be like Jesus. And yet it seems so out of my reach, so impossible. How can we, mere human beings, be expected to match ourselves against the Son of God? He has an utterly unfair start on us.'

'I know we are told he was "truly and properly man", and that he was tempted in all points like us, but you can't get away from the fact that he was different. He was divine. He wasn't really one of us at all. So, isn't it a bit unreasonable to expect us to be like him? To tell you the truth, it is not so much a hope that possesses me as a feeling of hopelessness.'

The dilemma is real enough. A considerable strand of New Testament teaching and the thrust of most holiness preaching is that our lives should reflect the actions, attitudes and thinking of our Lord Jesus, and that our constant aim should be to become more and more like him. We feel intuitively that this is right and we long for it in the depths of our personality. But the difficulty lies in that he was the *Lord* Jesus and, as Christian teaching encapsules it, he was truly and properly God—and we are not. And the more we speak of him and worship him as the incarnate Son of God the further removed he seems to become from us. Wonderful and glorious, yes. But one of us, no. And to be like him, a nice sentiment but quite unrealistic.

Is there a way out of this dilemma? Is there a way that Jesus can be seen as one of us and not as a God-man who could call to his aid divine powers unavailable to us?

The orthodox answer that he is both God and man at the same time is a statement of faith and does not pretend to satisfy the mind with a rational explanation as to how this could be. Attempts to expand on the basic statement have invariably echoed one or other of the historical heresies in that they have emphasised one aspect at the expense of the other. And yet, there is a way—a way towards being able to identify ourselves with the man Jesus. It is this. In addition to the obvious human characteristics that we share with Jesus, there is a further common denominator between us: the presence and power of the Holy Spirit in his life and ours. What we know in part he experienced in all its fullness. What we have experienced incompletely and imperfectly—he experienced perfectly. But there is a bond between us. He is the Man perfectly filled with the Spirit. We are but beginners, our experience is imperfect—but it is the same Spirit we share.

Of course, to say that Jesus was the Man perfectly filled with the Spirit can in no way hope to exhaust the depth of meaning of the incarnation. But from the rarefied air of the world which the theologians inhabit comes the message that God is giving his children a new insight. The way forward, the path to understanding of the dual nature of Christ, lies in further exploration of the doctrine of the Holy Spirit.

But to return to the realm of practical living, it is clear that the concept of Jesus as the Man perfectly filled with the Spirit, and ourselves as men and women partially filled, opens doors to new insights when it comes to our understanding of the Christlike life. It makes Jesus our brother. We share the same nature. He is one of us. He may be in the first division, and we in the second—and far down the league table at that—but we are of a kind, and the same purpose engages us. He may be at the summit of the mountain while we are still in the foothills—but the resources which were his are ours as well.

One consequence of looking at Jesus as the Man perfectly filled with the Spirit is that every detail of his daily life and experience takes on a new significance. Just how did 'Jesus of Nazareth, a man singled out by God and made known to you through miracles, portents, and signs, which God worked among you through him' (Acts 2:22), come to experience the Holy Spirit in his life—and what does that tell us about our own approach to God? What difference did the presence of the Holy Spirit make to him—and to us? How did it affect his character and his mission? And what kind of a man is the Man who is perfectly filled with the Spirit? How did

Christ act, react, respond, think and feel in any given situation—and what does it teach us, who are but imperfectly filled, about Spirit-inspired actions, reactions, responses, thoughts and feelings in our daily lives? What was Jesus really like?

At the beginning of this century Albert Schweitzer put a virtual end to the writing of biographies of Jesus when he demonstrated in *The Quest of the Historical Jesus* that the many biographies written up to that time revealed more of the presuppositions, ideals, values and even natures of the writers themselves than of their subject. The gospels simply do not give us sufficient material to construct a full life of Jesus in the style of a modern biography, which seeks to explore deeply into the psychology of the person, the development of his thinking and the interaction upon him of the various events and influences of his life. About the first 30 years we know next to nothing, and even the years of his ministry are only partially reported.

But what the gospels do give us is a series of glimpses of the man—descriptions of his actions, reports of his words, the comments of those looking on—and each glimpse has something to tell us about him. By analysing the drop of water we discover the nature of the ocean. If in this particular situation the man perfectly filled with the Spirit responded in this particular way—what does that tell me about him, and therefore about me?

We shall be looking at a number of such life situations as recorded in the New Testament, with the purpose of seeking to understand more fully what it means to live a holy, Christlike, Spirit-filled and effective life. The quest for the seeker after truth is by no means hopeless. The clue lies in the last part of the chorus:

To be like Jesus—this hope possesses me,
His Spirit helping me
Like him I'll be.

2

Jesus—armed with the Spirit

WE are so used to hearing 'before and after' testimonies in terms of sinners being transformed by the power of God, that it comes as a surprise to realise that Jesus of Nazareth had a kind of 'before and after' testimony to give. At the age of 30 his life was to take a new, dramatic turn through an experience of the Spirit. The details are sparse. There is no personal recollection by Jesus to quote about his thoughts and feelings during the time leading up to the event, no moment by moment description of what happened to him then and afterwards. The record simply says that 'during a general baptism of the people, when Jesus too had been baptised and was praying, heaven opened and the Holy Spirit descended on him in bodily form like a dove; and there came a voice from heaven, "Thou art my Son, my Beloved; on thee my favour rests"' (Luke 3:21, 22).

But Luke interprets the significance of the event for us. 'Full of the Holy Spirit,' he says, 'Jesus returned from the Jordan, and for forty days was led by the Spirit up and down the wilderness and tempted by the devil' (Luke 4:1, 2). And he continues: 'Then Jesus, armed with the power of the Spirit, returned to Galilee' (Luke 4:14). It is in this return to his home town that we get a revealing glimpse of the transformation that had taken place in him. 'He came to Nazareth, where he had been brought up,' Luke tells us, 'and went to synagogue on the Sabbath day as he regularly did.'

There was an air of expectancy—word had travelled that something remarkable had happened to Joseph's son. 'He stood up to read the lesson . . . "The spirit of the Lord is upon me because he has anointed me. . . ." He rolled up the scroll, gave it back to the attendant, and sat down; and all eyes in the synagogue were fixed on him.' The atmosphere was electric. After a moment 'He began to speak: "Today", he said, "in your very hearing this text has come true.'' There was a general stir of admiration; they were surprised that words of such grace should fall from his lips' (4:16-23).

'''Where does he get it from?'' they said, and, ''What wisdom is this that has been given him?'', and, ''How does he work such miracles? Is not this the carpenter, the son of Mary, the brother of James and Joseph and Judas and Simon? And are not his sisters here with us?''' (Mark 6: 2, 3). Something had happened to the young man they had known all these years. It was still the carpenter who stood before them—but he was different. Very different.

Bradford is a long way from Nazareth and the scene which Michael Harper describes in *As at the Beginning* occurs 19 centuries later, but again it is a craftsman, this time a plumber, who has the audience gripped. 'His wife Polly normally did all the talking, but this time she was sitting critically at the back. ''This will teach him a lesson,'' she had said to herself, ''claiming to be more baptised in the Spirit than me. . . .'' She'd be there to see him make a fool of himself. That would soon knock some sense into him.

'He spoke from the text that Jesus read when he returned to his home church after his experience of power at the River Jordan. . . . The eyes of that critical audience were riveted on Jesus, and now the same thing was happening in a Bradford chapel. He usually sat meekly, beside his wife while she harangued the people in her dynamic way, but now he was on his feet facing at least one strong critic. Polly became more and more agitated as he went on, until, unable to contain herself any longer, she cried out in a voice that many could hear: ''That's not my Smith, Lord, that's not my Smith.'''

But it *was* her Smith, it was still the plumber that everyone had known. And yet he was different. Very different. Smith Wigglesworth would be the last to claim that exactly what had happened to Jesus had happened to him—for it is only 'in Christ that the complete being of the Godhead dwells embodied' (Colossians 2:9). But he would be the first to say that by the grace of God he had been privileged to experience to a degree and imperfectly what Jesus had experienced fully and perfectly. Both had become empowered by the Holy Spirit and both commissioned to a ministry.

God does not only visit the sinner with transforming power. He visits the believer too. Many of the most startling accounts of personal transformation refer not to non-Christians finding grace but to ordinary, devout, practising Christians being changed into extraordinary disciples, full of the Holy Spirit.

To mention but two instances. Francis of Assisi, a high-spirited young man, impulsive but intermittent in his devotion to God, enters the little church of Saint Damiano and kneels before the crucifix to pray. And, in the simple words of the biographer of old, 'having been smitten by unwonted visitations, found himself another man than he who had gone in'.

John Wesley, an anglican clergyman, in William Sangster's phrases: 'a man disciplined in virtue and constantly on the stretch for the highest; marvellously equipped but pitifully ineffective', enters a meeting in Aldersgate Street. As he listens to the reading of Luther's preface to Romans his heart becomes 'strangely warmed'. He leaves the meeting a transformed man, a man who within a short time will turn England upside down through his preaching.

What is it that releases these mighty inpourings of the Spirit in the heart of the believer, and can everyone expect to be so visited? The guideposts in the New Testament and subsequent Christian teaching regarding initial conversion, salvation as Saul of Tarsus experienced, are abundant and clear. But when it comes to the transforming experiences that change the ordinary believer into saint and hero the road is less well mapped. The New Testament has surprisingly little to tell us about these extraordinary divine visitations. In various traditions, and especially from the time of John Wesley onwards, elaborate doctrinal structures have been built up which seek to chart the way for the seeking pilgrim. But the element of mystery and unpredictability remains.

Why was Jesus filled with the Spirit at the age of 30, and why was Francis of Assisi empowered at the age of 24 and Wesley at 36? What subtle chemistry of soul and mind determined that? Or was the timing God's? How is it that for some the divine baptism comes unexpectedly—out of the blue—as a man stumbling across treasure in a field? And how is it that for others the experience comes only after a long, sometimes agonising searching for the goodly pearl? And why is it that for some the longed for and yearned after spiritual breakthrough seems never to come?

There are, of course, tentative and not so tentative answers that can be given to those questions, but as John V. Taylor puts it, we need to be 'as ready as the weather forecaster to admit that however reliable our calculations most of the time, we cannot command the wind'. It is important, though, that we differentiate between these mighty inrushings of Holy Spirit power and the reception of the Holy Spirit himself. The gift of the Holy Spirit is the birthright of every Christian. 'The promise is to you, and to your children, and to all who are far away, everyone whom the Lord our God may call' (Acts 2:39). It is by definition the Spirit's presence that makes a person a Christian, for 'if a man does not possess the Spirit of Christ, he is no Christian' (Romans 8:9).

Soon as my all I ventured on the atoning Blood,
The Holy Spirit entered, and I was born of God.

And the believer who yearns for a great inpouring of divine power, and who believes that the yearning has been implanted within him by God himself, keeps his heart ever open before the Lord in quiet expectation. He treasures the measure of the Spirit he has already received, and his hands and mind remain active in the service of the Lord, but in the secret places of his soul he keeps the room ever ready for the guest of the soul who could come at any time.

3

A remarkably original man

WHAT was Jesus of Nazareth, the Man perfectly filled with the Spirit, really like? One answer is that he was a man remarkably himself. He was no copy of anyone else. He was a true original. Saints have frequently had a disconcerting way of marching to the sound of drums that only they could hear, and one does not have to look far in the pages of the gospels to find that the Man perfectly filled with the Spirit disturbed those around him by his sheer originality. If he was a prophet—why did he not dress and live like one? If he was a teacher of the law—why those disconcerting additions: 'But *I* say unto you . . .'? If he was a religious man—why did he associate with the wrong people?

The uncertain fate of the passage which describes the incident in the Temple in which Jesus utters the 'unutterable' to the woman taken in adultery: 'Neither do I condemn thee' (John 8:2-11, *AV*), bears signs of the Early Church feeling distinctly uncomfortable with the startling originality of its founder. That Jesus did not condemn the woman must have come as a shock to his contemporaries steeped in the law and tradition. 'This passage', comments the panel of scholars responsible for the *New English Bible* translation, 'has no fixed place in our ancient witnesses. Some of them do not contain it at all. Some place it after Luke 21:38, others after John 7:36, or John 7:52, or John 21:24.' An early instance of orthodoxy trying to muzzle nonconformity?

The Salvation Army does not canonise its saints, but who could doubt that George Scott Railton would be a leading contender if it did? In the saints certain of the characteristics of the Spirit-filled life are seen in magnified form, and to the despair of William and Bramwell Booth, Railton could not be pinned down or made to conform. He was uniquely himself. None present would ever forget the scene in Queen's Hall when Railton made his public protest against The Salvation Army's new assurance society—which to him was a standing denial of our Lord's charge not to lay up treasure on earth. Bernard Watson describes the scene in *Soldier Saint*:

> William Booth was in charge. Railton entered at the last moment and took his place on the platform, barefooted and dressed in sackcloth—just like a friar. Just like Railton! With no hint of what was to follow Booth joined in the general applause. Everyone loved Railton's eccentric gestures; all knew that he was a holy man. Dear Railton! One never knew what he would be doing next.

What he did next caused quite a furore. When opportunity for testimony was given, Railton stood on his feet and pulling from his pocket a life assurance advertisement proceeded to let everyone know what he thought about the offer made on that 'dirty piece of paper'. 'It is inviting our officers', he thundered, 'to pay 20 shillings of the Lord's money and offering to give them 33 farthings yearly in return—a farthing for each year of Christ's life on earth.' As a final flourish he placed the paper solemnly on the floor and then trampled on it.

Perhaps Bernard Watson understates the case when he reports that 'William Booth was embarrassed and many headquarters officers were shocked'! But what has this somewhat extreme example of originality to say to us who would not claim to be Railtons? It has something immensely important to say. One of the instinctive fears of the human spirit is that by opening itself up to the fount of spiritual life it will have to become conformed to a particular 'religious' type of personality. Many people carry round in their minds a caricature of what a Spirit-filled person should be like—narrow, rigid, self-righteous, drab—and they recoil from this stereotype. This picture reflects Swinburne's bitter cry: 'Thou hast conquered, O pale Galilean; the world has grown grey from Thy breath', and the human spirit shies away from the prospect of losing its colour and individuality. 'Must I really become like that?' we ask in horror.

The answer is a glorious no. Each of us is a unique, individual self, and we honour the creator God, not by seeking to conform to a type, however worthy, or by trying to be someone we are not, but by the measure that we learn to become our true selves and strive to reach our highest God-given potential.

Now, quite contrary to popular suspicion, the experience of the saints is that they have most become themselves as they have allowed the Spirit of God to break in on them. The Holy Spirit does not come to destroy but to enhance our nature. Not to repress but to help us express ourselves. He is not competing against the creator God—he *is* the creator God. At no time is a man more himself than when he is in Christ. This is not a plea for rampant individualism. Every truth has its complementary truth. And the other and equally valid side of the picture is that God gives different gifts to different people and that our gifts need to be pooled if the Church is to be built up.

But we need to guard against the many and subtle pressures around us that would squeeze us into their moulds—often with the very best of intentions. What, for example, could be more worthily motivated than the programme at Salvation Army training colleges to turn new cadets into 'good officers'? During training days an identikit picture of the 'ideal officer' may be formed, perhaps containing a strong element of William Booth, a touch of Catherine, a dash of Railton and a pinch of Brengle—not to mention the seasoning of the members of staff and visiting officers. But by the end of the session, if the cadet is of a sensitive nature, this idealised picture may have so firmly impressed itself upon his mind that he will be in danger of going through life with a permanent inferiority complex—for the ideal officer is superb at everything and does nothing indifferently!

With what relief comes the discovery that God has not called us to be William Booth, or Railton, or that splendid salvationist at my corps who somehow makes me feel so inadequate whenever he gives his testimony. How comforting to realise that he wants me to be me, and yet how challenging at the same time! For, in the words of the old Jewish saying, on the great judgment day God will not say, 'Why were you not Moses?' He will say, 'Why were you not yourself?'

4

A remarkably authoritative man

THE remarkable authority of the Man perfectly filled with the Spirit made a deep impression on his contemporaries. They were 'astonished at the way he taught,' comments Matthew (7:28, *Barclay*), 'for he taught as one who needed no authority beyond his own, and not like the experts in the Law.' Other prophets had said, 'Thus says the Lord.' Jesus said, 'I say to you.'

He had authority over evil spirits. When in the synagogue he commanded the unclean spirit to come out of the man, and it did, 'they were all dumbfounded and began to ask one another, "What is this? A new kind of teaching! He speaks with authority. When he gives orders, even the unclean spirits submit"' (Mark 1:27). His authority extended even to the elements. When he stood up in the storm-tossed boat and 'rebuked the wind and the sea . . . there was a dead calm. The men were astonished at what had happened, and exclaimed, "What sort of man is this? Even the wind and the sea obey him"' (Matthew 8:26, 27).

But more than that; his very presence commanded authority. One of the tensest moments in the ministry of Jesus occurred early when he was visiting his home town of Nazareth. After the initial reaction of surprise and admiration the crowd in the synagogue turned hostile. 'At these words,' records Luke, 'the whole congregation were infuriated. They leapt up, threw him out of the town, and took him to the brow of the hill on which it was built, meaning to hurl him over the edge' (4:28-30). The mob was ready to lynch him, but something about him, some aura of divine power around him, made them hold back. As Luke continues, 'he walked straight through them all, and went away.' On another occasion, 'as soon as they saw Jesus the whole crowd were overcome with awe' (Mark 9:15).

Even his disciples were not immune to the feeling. 'They were on the road, going up to Jerusalem, Jesus leading the way; and the disciples were filled with awe, while those who followed behind were afraid' (Mark 10:32). He spoke with authority, he acted with authority, his presence communicated authority. There was no doubt about it: he was a man of astonishing authority.

In his pioneer work *The Idea of the Holy,* Rudolf Otto had to coin a new word, the sense of the 'numinous', to describe the mixture of awe, fear and yet fascination with which primitive man approached the divine—feelings which still lie deeply buried within us all. He chose to invent a new term because the word 'holy' had changed in meaning over the centuries. We now use it to describe goodness, ethical excellence, moral perfection. But in its original meaning it was this element of the numinous which predominated—the sense of awe-inspiring mystery and yet fearful fascination. Anything that had come into contact with God or had been set aside for him, whether person, thing, place or day, was holy—it was touched with the numinous. Only very gradually during the period spanned by the Old Testament did the words holy and holiness take on the deep, additional meaning of ethical goodness and, later, through the revelation of Jesus, that of love.

But if in encounters with the divine throughout the ages the human soul has instinctively felt a sense of fascinated awe, it comes as no surprise to discover that when people met the most holy, the most God-filled man ever to have lived, they too sensed that they were in the presence of the numinous: they felt intuitively that here was a man of God. His words were imbued with eternal meaning, miraculous powers irradiated from him, and there was that unfathomable dimension about him, that indefinable authority of his, that created within one a sense of awe. And yet, at the same time, one could not help being fascinated, even attracted by him.

Authority without winsomeness would have made the Man perfectly filled with the Spirit a forbidding figure. But in Jesus, as William Sangster comments in *The Pure in Heart,* 'every virtue is balanced with its complementary virtue! The vices of good men are often shadows cast by their virtues. Because they are so morally strong, they lack tenderness. Because they are so generous, a proper prudence is wanting. But in Jesus the balance and harmony are all there.'

Spiritual authority is a mark of the Spirit-filled man. When the diminutive David Wilkerson faced the members of the Chaplains, reputedly one of the toughest gangs in New York, on a street corner in Fort Greene, Brooklyn, he needed all the divine authority he could get. It was impossible to get a hearing—so he simply bowed his head and prayed. After a few moments the change began and, when he looked up, he saw that not only had the smaller children settled down, but 'that a lot of the older boys who had been leaning up against the school fence, smoking, had straightened up, taken their hats off and were now standing with their heads slightly bowed'. 'I was so startled by the sudden silence,' he comments, 'that I was at a loss for words.' After speaking to them on John 3:16, David asked to meet their leaders. They came forward. Sensing by their comments that something he had said had 'got through' to them, he quietly said to the leaders: 'I want you to kneel down right here in the street and ask the Holy Spirit to come into your lives so that you will become new men, new creatures in Christ.'

No scene in *The Cross and the Switchblade* is more dramatic. 'There was a long pause. For the first time I was vaguely aware of the crowd that was waiting, very quietly, to see what was going to happen. Finally Stagecoach said, in a voice that was strangely hoarse: "Buckboard? You want to? I will if you will." And before my astonished eyes, these two leaders of one of the most feared fighting gangs in all of New York slowly dropped to their knees.' They may not have been able to express it in so many words, but they had felt the same sense of numinous in the country preacher. His words and his presence had the imprint of spiritual authority.

Spiritual authority is a powerful weapon—and a dangerous one—that God entrusts to his servants. It is a gift, a compound quality made up of many elements, but a gift that cannot be sought directly without becoming grotesque. It is the by-product of the Spirit's indwelling and it is the fullness of that indwelling which must be the object of our seeking. Any resulting influence may safely be left with him, for nothing is less Christlike than a continual looking over the shoulder to see what impression is being made. But it is a dangerous weapon in that he in whom divine powers are released becomes a prime target for the tempter. Spiritual arrogance is a close cousin to spiritual authority.

But no understanding of holy living which leaves out the dynamic quality of the Spirit's work in and through us is adequate. Holy living is more than a quest for ethical perfection. It is also an opening of the personality to the mighty forces of the Spirit in order to mediate them to a needy world.

5

A remarkably attractive man

THOUGH there had been no prophets for many centuries when John the Baptist appeared in the desert, he matched exactly the popular expectation of what a man of God should be. Dour, abstemious, condemnatory, evoking fear and respect—the very image of the prophets of old. But when the prophet Jesus, the Man perfectly filled with the Spirit, began his ministry he took everyone by surprise. Direct, even harsh at times, he evoked awe and respect. But what stood out supremely was the winsomeness of the man. Here was an outgoing, attractive personality who rejoiced in the company of others and enjoyed the good things of life. Children felt at ease with him and even the social outcasts of the day were invited to share his table. You couldn't help warming to him. He was so delightfully human!

The contrast between Jesus and his group, and John and his followers, was so marked that in the end John's disciples came to him with the question: 'Why do we and the Pharisees fast, but your disciples do not?' To this Jesus cheerfully and disconcertingly replied, 'Can you expect the bridegroom's friends to go mourning while the bridegroom is with them?' (Matthew 9:14, 15). On another occasion Jesus himself remarked on the difference between his cousin and himself. 'John came, neither eating nor drinking, and they say, "He is possessed." The Son of Man came eating and drinking, and they say, "Look at him! a glutton and a drinker, a friend of tax-gatherers and sinners!"' (Matthew 11:18, 19).

The fact that the Man perfectly filled with the Spirit was such a warm and engaging personality, so extraordinarily human in the best sense of that word, and so obviously at home in his Father's world, is a point of great importance for us who are seeking to learn from him.

In the Early Church two contrasting strands of Christianity emerged, strands which have developed over the centuries and which have influenced us all personally. The labels usually given to these differing approaches to the faith are life (or world) affirming and life (or world) denying. The first takes Jesus as its model and highlights the beauty and goodness of that which God has created for our enjoyment and enrichment. The second could be said to take John the Baptist as its patron saint and emphasises the need to withdraw and be separate from the created world if we are to be truly spiritual.

An unfortunate synthesis of the two viewpoints was achieved early in Christian history whereby it was held that the life affirming approach was all right for the ordinary believer, but if one wanted to be perfect (based on our Lord's words to the rich young ruler: 'If you wish to go the whole way . . .' (Matthew 19:21)) then one had to embrace life denial and separate oneself from the world. This had the effect of dividing Christianity into first and second class, professional and amateur Christians, and influenced the monastic movement.

Though protestant thought has on the whole been life affirming, holiness teaching has sometimes betrayed a life denying streak and become synonymous with Paul's use of Isaiah's prophetic call to the Israelites to leave Babylon: 'Come out from among them, and be ye separate, saith the Lord' (2 Corinthians 6:17, *AV*). The list of things which believers at sundry times have been urged to separate themselves from makes sad reading. It includes fiction, especially novels, drama, art, sport, leisure, fashion, the cinema, the theatre, non-Christian companionships, higher education, tasty food. And the general suspicion of advances in scientific knowledge which is characteristic of the life denying approach is illustrated by the fact that radio, television and the study of psychology have to be added to the list. With however much sympathetic understanding one reads such a catalogue one cannot help feeling that it reflects more of John the Baptist than of Jesus of Nazareth.

The trouble with the life denying world view is that it fails to distinguish between the good and beautiful world God created, and the streak of evil and pain which is undoubtedly there as well. The germ of second-century Gnostic teaching, that all created matter is inherently evil, is still around, despite being roundly condemned as heretical, and from time to time causes an infection to break out. Those who deny the world feel that it is so bad that it has to be written off, whereas those who affirm its glory in God's creation and all its latent God-given possibilities reject only the evil streak. In terms of daily living it is not always easy to draw the precise boundary line between the good world and the evil within it—hence some of the incongruities we have noted above. But to write off the world as a whole is to write off the creator God and his handiwork, something which, significantly, the Man perfectly filled with the Spirit refused to do. And the life denying approach rejects not only the world and society around us, it rejects human nature as well. It is not to be trusted. By nature man is unclean, unworthy, insignificant, and his every motive, ambition, drive and instinct suspect.

But teaching which stresses the worm-likeness of man stands in curious contrast to the high view of human nature which Jesus seemingly had. It remains one of the stunning facts about the synoptic gospels that in presenting the exalted ethical ideals of the Kingdom of God, Jesus did not feel it necessary to make the kind of allowance for human inability and weakness which Paul was subsequently to make, and which Augustine five centuries later developed into a doctrine of man's total depravity. It was as if Jesus expected mankind as a matter of course to be able to live up to the ideals he was proclaiming. This does not mean that he was unaware of the flaw in human nature, but rather that he chose to highlight the image of God in man which undoubtedly is also there.

Too much stress on the corruption of our nature is an implied criticism of the God who made us. For, as H. A. Williams comments in *The True Wilderness,* 'the idea that we should do God honour by the constant denigration of ourselves is as absurd as the idea that the way to compliment a parent is to tell him how horrible his children are'. Too much stress on the corruption of our nature can also lead us astray in our quest after Christlike lives. For if my human nature is the anti-Christ, then I must fight, oppose, reject, refuse, repress, exterminate it. Do anything but identify with it. The only real me I can permit is the spiritual me. But the end result is inevitable. If we refuse to identify ourselves with our humanity we condemn ourselves to becoming lopsided, crippled, milk and water personalities, devoid of that engaging wholesomeness which made Jesus so attractive a person. Joseph Conrad describes one of his characters as 'prayerfully divesting himself of the last vestiges of humanity'—a devastating caricature of defective Christian teaching, for if my human nature is God-given then the last thing I must do is to seek to divest myself of it. On the contrary, I must open myself more fully to the God who made me so that he can enhance and perfect what is his. And if the world around me, with all its exciting opportunities and challenges, is also God-given I must not try to escape from it, but must open myself to every wholesome experience that life offers, whilst at the same time praying for the divine insight that will help me to identify the evil streak both within myself and the world in order to reject it.

And now we come full circle. When human beings reject their environment and seek to live on a purely spiritual plane, the net result is that they become unreal, desiccated, less than full-blooded human personalities—and strangely unattractive. But when, like the Man perfectly filled with the Spirit, they give themselves fully to their God-created environment and rejoice in their humanity, their personalities come alive and glow—which, in the case of Jesus, proved extraordinarily attractive.

6

A remarkably uncompromising man

BODY language can sometimes speak more eloquently than words. In Mark, we get a rare glimpse of the physical reaction of Jesus to a challenge. When he had explained to his disciples that he had to suffer and die, 'Peter took him by the arm and began to rebuke him. But Jesus turned round' (or as Barclay, seeking to bring out the decisiveness of the action in the original, puts it: 'Jesus swung round,') 'and, looking at his disciples, rebuked Peter. "Away with you, Satan," he said, "you think as men think, not as God thinks."' (8:32, 33). That the physical response of Jesus has been preserved in the accounts of this incident shows how indelible was the impression left by our Lord suddenly wrenching himself free from Peter's arm around him and turning sharply to face the group. Why was this physical reaction followed by some of the strongest words Jesus ever spoke to a friend? It would appear that Peter had unwittingly touched a sensitive spot.

The temptation in the desert to take the easy way in his ministry, to court popularity and win men's minds by dazzling displays of supernatural powers, was no once-and-for-all experience. The thought must have been continually at the back of his mind, and Luke, in fact, says that 'the devil departed, biding his time' (Luke 4:13). Now here he was, back again with the same suggestion, only this time it was even harder for he was using Peter as his spokesman. But our Lord's reaction was swift and spontaneous. The suggestion was instantly rejected with almost explosive force by gesture and word.

Our Lord's most frequent command to his disciples was that they were to 'watch!' to 'keep awake', so that they would not be caught out and fall into temptation. This undoubtedly reflected his own experience. And it was not only a matter of being on guard—anything that could come between a man and his God had to be ruthlessly rejected. His commitment was absolute. He taught others that if it was an eye that was their undoing it was better to tear it out, and that if it was a hand they were to cut it off and fling it away, and in the end he himself chose to die rather than to yield his commitment to God and his will for him.

If the Man perfectly filled with the Spirit was so acutely sensitive to the downward pull of sin and felt the need to be constantly on guard and was prepared to go to any lengths, even the forfeiting of his life, to reject it, how much more ought we to 'keep awake', we who have but a fraction of his strength. It is a mistake to think that when we open ourselves to the Spirit of God the spiritual battle is over. In a sense it only then begins. Opening the door to the wind of Heaven exposes us to other, less welcome, blasts as well. The heightened awareness of things spiritual, which is one of the blessings of the Spirit's presence, brings as its inevitable concomitant a heightened awareness of the power of evil. We can be quite sure that Jesus had never before known such spiritual turmoil as he experienced in the desert *after* the power of the Spirit had come upon him. And if, for the believer, Paul's words about fighting 'not against human foes, but against cosmic powers' (Ephesians 6:12) might previously have seemed tinged with poetic licence, they now take on a fearful reality. The price of being alive in the Spirit is that we become alive to evil as well.

If the flaw within human nature could be identified and removed, like taking out a rotten tooth, how simple it would be to 'keep awake'. But that cannot be. We are fearfully and wonderfully made and every part of us has potential for good or ill. Our instincts—whether of flight, repulsion, curiosity, pugnacity, self-abasement, self-assertion, sex, gregariousness, or any other—our emotions, our will, our conscious and subconscious minds and any of the other factors which make us tick as human beings—are all God-given and are therefore meant to reflect the image of the Creator, but they are also all potential trouble points.

And if the evil streak in the world could be isolated how much easier it would be to 'watch'—but that is also plainly impossible. Leaving aside the self-evident evils with which we are surrounded, there remains a huge strata of life which is not self-evidently right or wrong. On many of the great issues, like war, abortion, euthanasia, cloning, there will be honest divergences of opinions among Christians. On other issues, what may be right for one man may be wrong for another—motivation often being the key factor. There are few blacks and whites in situational ethics.

Keeping on guard, therefore, is no simple matter, and when one considers the human mind's capacity for self-deception and rationalisation, it can only be with relief that we remember that one of the Holy Spirit's specific functions is to show where wrong and right and judgment lie (John 16:8) and that he, 'who is the Spirit of truth . . . will guide you into all the truth' (John 16:13).

It is a measure of our Lord's stature that he was able to take such a positive view of the world and human nature while at the same time being ruthless with anything that would put his relationship with God at risk. Lesser souls, as we have already noted, have felt it necessary to try to escape from it all but Jesus trusted his Spirit-enhanced powers of discernment.

The tempter will attack us on our strong points, for every step forward in faith and obedience is an affront to him. We must expect and prepare for the counter-attack. By every subtle means at his disposal he will try to make us lessen our commitment, make us compromise, settle down, draw back again. How easily even the purest gold becomes mixed with dross! Perhaps it is significant that Albert Orsborn received more letters about his song, 'Saviour, if my feet have faltered on the pathway of the cross', than any other—and that the song was written out of a painful experience that taught him that 'when the Spirit grieves he leaves'.

But the tempter will also attack us on our weak points—and where is the human being who has none of these? Some of our weaknesses are the result of deliberate choices on our part, while others—like some of our innate fears, inhibitions, complexes and 'structural weaknesses'—are the consequences of inherited traits or early environmental circumstances. But the tempter knows them all.

Mrs Commissioner Olive Holbrook tells of the astonished reaction of the congregation at the corps she attended as a young girl, when a saintly, elderly local officer thanked God in a testimony, that despite persistent temptation over the period of his whole life he had never yielded to the one great temptation of his life: to drink alcohol. People turned to each other in amazement. Drink? The very last thing one would have imagined could have been a testing point in his life! But the revered old man went on to explain his mother had died as an incurable alcoholic—but her weakness had been passed on to him in the bloodstream. At times the craving for alcohol had racked his body and mind as if an unknown, seemingly irresistible, force was compelling him to yield—but he never had.

Perhaps for him too it was with a mighty physical wrench that he had torn himself free and swung round to hurl at his tormentor: 'Away with you, Satan!'

7

A remarkably effective man

THAT the old saying about being too heavenly-minded to be of any earthly use remains in vogue is probably because many think it has the ring of truth. Everyone knows that Buddha-like contemplation of one's navel is hardly in the Christian tradition, but the impression is nevertheless around that a truly holy man is a contemplative who ponders the universe—not a man of action. A lovely person, we say, but so impractical, something of a saint, really. The fortuitous circumstance that one of the Army's best-known and loved exponents of the holy life, Commissioner Samuel Brengle, found organisational work uncongenial has tended to reinforce the same impression within salvationist circles. An activist saint? A doer, an organiser, a leader, a dynamic thruster? A contradiction in terms!

And yet Jesus, the Man perfectly filled with the Spirit, was just that: an activist, and a remarkably effective man. His schedule was crowded. 'He went round the whole of Galilee,' reports Matthew, 'teaching in the synagogues, preaching the gospel of the Kingdom, and curing whatever illness or infirmity there was among the people' (Matthew 4:23). He gave interviews to individuals, spent some time training his disciples, settled their quarrels, kept his eye on the purse and food situation, had hard-headed answers for trick questioners, and was constantly on the move so that every town could be covered. He had energy and drive. The authorities feared him as a revolutionary leader. He was a man of action.

What does this say to us who are but partially filled with the Spirit? Is the man of God always an activist? The answer to that is a qualified yes—for here we must note an important qualification regarding the phrase, 'to be like Jesus'. It is only possible and only desirable up to a point to try to be like him—as the next paragraph will explain.

More than 400 years before Christ, Hippocrates divided mankind into four broad strata of temperaments, and said that our personalities could be classified according to whether they were predominantly sanguine, choleric, melancholy or phlegmatic. Most temperaments would have more than one element—but one could be said to predominate. Though the actual terms coined by Hippocrates are not used so much today, psychologists nevertheless continue to distinguish types of personality, on the basis, say, of whether the rational or emotional factors are the salient ones, or whether the person is mainly introverted or extroverted.

It follows from this that the man Jesus of Nazareth must also have had certain characteristic personality traits—and this in turn has a bearing on our seeking to be 'like him'. For if a person who is predominantly phlegmatic, to use Hippocrates' categories, seeks slavishly to emulate the man Jesus, whose basic temperament included a strong sanguine content, he is doomed to defeat and frustration. Our imitation of Christ must be in the context of our personality—a seeking to express the values we see in him, through what we ourselves are, not an outward imitation that strains our basic temperament.

With due regard, then, to the differences of temperaments, the mistaken popular perception of the holy man as a passive personality needs correcting. If holiness is associated with inactivity and ineffectiveness it will have little appeal, and rightly so. And if we call saints only those who live cloistered, contemplative lives, we shall miss seeing the halo in the multitude of activist saints who have pulled up their sleeves and grappled with the multifarious business of everyday living. One has only to call the roll of the great saints of the past to realise how mistaken is the impression of ineffectiveness. Both Peter and Paul were men of action whose dynamic personalities forged the Early Church. Augustine had to try to snatch the time he needed for his writing from his demanding duties as a bishop—which in those days was like being a local mayor, teacher, doctor, judge and priest rolled into one.

Take the great Catherine of Siena. Evelyn Underhill describes her as a 'great active and a great ecstatic; at once politician, teacher and contemplative, holding a steady balance between the inner and outer life. Well named "the mother of a thousand souls", with little education she yet contrived, in a short career dogged by persistent ill health, to change the course of history, rejuvenate religion, and compose, in her "Divine Dialogue", one of the jewels of Italian religious literature.' And of her namesake of Genoa, the founder of hospitals as we know them today, Evelyn Underhill coins the lovely epithet, 'an indomitable doer'.

Consider John Wesley. Pre-eminent as evangelist, preacher, organiser and church leader, he was up at four every morning to press on with the great task that took him on horseback throughout England, addressing meeting after meeting in the open air, while in between guiding and settling the affairs of methodism. His life has been judged as 'the busiest and, in some respects, the most important life of the 18th century'.

When we come to the ranks of salvationists it becomes difficult to single out any particular individual, for drive and activism has been the hallmark of the salvationist saint throughout. But by way of illustration, here are some extracts from the list that Commissioner Karl Larsson, a 'viking warrior of old', jotted down of the things he had done on a 'typical day'—3 March 1910—when he was chief secretary in Sweden:

> Saw trade secretary re new employee—saw training principal re courtship of Cadet B and Captain W—checked self-denial letter and sent it to printer—saw Adjutant Lund re selling of a new book—dealt with letter from Mariestad re lost boy—dealt with letter from Captain H re her appointment—dealt with letter from London re rate of exchange—prepared lecture for cadets—gave one hour's lecture to cadets—drafted letter re oversight of local officers—saw trade secretary regarding Adjutant N's journey home—saw organising secretary re singer's tour and staff band—dealt with phone call from police complaining about posters—saw Major Grewell re birth-certificates for three missionaries—saw Adjutant Karlson re complaints about staff band meetings—saw social secretary re requesting for collecting boxes by political party—interviewed salvationist applying for job—saw Ensign Wacht re supplies from wholesaler—wrote Stockholm COs re ending of soup distribution—wrote weekly *War Cry* column and delivered it to printer—dealt with letter from V re link with teetotal group—saw Mr Ringt re donation—proof read *The War Cry*—gave two hours of classes to cadets—interviewed Captain Broberg—two hours—saw financial secretary for two hours on business matters—corrected the cadet sergeants' sermon outlines.

And to conclude that a man that busy could not possibly have been a saint is to draw entirely the wrong conclusion, for the Holy Spirit is a Spirit of energy; a dynamic, creative force that enhances the natural powers of the personality. And as the believer gives the Spirit increasingly free reign within his personality so those traditional energy-absorbers of guilt, worry, anxiety, fear, inferiority, doubt, depression, indecisiveness, instability and restlessness lose their hold—releasing yet further physical, mental and spiritual energies within the personality. The man who is filled with the Spirit is dynamic.

And lest it should be thought that all of this applies only to those who are of predominantly sanguine temperament, let it be recorded that in his study of great men of the Bible from the angle of temperament, Tim LeHaye rates Peter as predominantly sanguine, Paul as predominantly choleric, Moses as mainly melancholic and Abraham as phlegmatic—and yet each in his own way was a doer, an achiever.

8

A remarkably serene man

THE daily life of Jesus was crowded with activity. The demands and pressures upon him were unceasing. But what stands out to the observer is that the Man perfectly filled with the Spirit was a remarkably serene personality. He moved from one task to the next with unhurried calm. He was not harassed, anxious, fretful. He was at peace. Mark describes the pressure: 'When they came ashore, he was immediately recognised; and the people scoured that whole countryside and brought the sick on stretchers to any place where he was reported to be. Wherever he went, to farmsteads, villages, or towns, they laid out the sick in the market-places and begged him to let them simply touch the edge of his cloak; and all who touched him were cured.' Jesus and the disciples 'had no leisure even to eat, so many were coming and going' (Mark 6:54-56, 31). On one occasion the crowd of people anxiously waiting to be healed by Jesus began building up even in the early hours and 'Simon and his companions searched him out' where he was praying in 'a lonely spot', and told him, 'They are all looking for you.'

Jesus was a deeply sensitive man who could be moved to tears by the sight of suffering, and in his mind he would have been able to picture the group awaiting him—the mother carrying her blind child in her arms, the father supporting his emaciated boy, the teen-ager cruelly lamed, the crippled girl—but with serenity of mind he replied to his disciples: 'Let us move on to the country towns in the neighbourhood; I have to proclaim my message there also; that is what I came out to do' (Mark 1:36-38).

The mental pressure of being unable to meet all the demands made on him would have reduced a lesser person to a nervous wreck. Here was no callous personality who at the flick of a switch could make the picture of suffering vanish from his mind. But he knew there were limits, human limits, to what he could accomplish. He would give himself to the very limit—but the rest he would have to leave quietly and without fretting to God.

Anyone who has engaged in a caring ministry will recognise the crushing, at times almost unbearable, burden of seeing suffering all around one and the feeling of utter hopelessness at being able to do so little about it. Michel Quoist speaks of it in his prayer, 'Lord, why did you tell me to love?' He describes how when he left the door of his heart ajar, people 'with outstretched hands, burning eyes and longing hearts' began crowding into his life in ever-increasing numbers:

> Now they have come from all over, in successive waves, pushing one another, jostling one another.
> They have come from all over town, from all parts of the country, of the world; numberless, inexhaustible.
> They don't come alone any longer but in groups, bound one to another;
> They come bending under heavy loads; loads of injustice, of resentment and hate, of suffering and sin . . .
> They drag the world behind them, with everything rusted, twisted, or badly adjusted.

And then the cry of pain, 'Lord, I can't stand it any more! It's too much!' And who has not shared that pain? The burden of the world crushes us. Our lives become anxious, weighed down with care—and even to talk about peace and serenity in such circumstances seems to us like escapism.

But it is not only the burden of a ministry which robs us of our inner serenity. In that spiritual classic, *A Testament of Devotion,* Thomas R. Kelly diagnoses the modern condition with such insight that it must be quoted at length:

> Our lives in a modern city grow too complex and overcrowded. Even the necessary obligations which we feel we must meet grow overnight, like Jack's beanstalk, and before we know it we are bowed down with burdens, crushed under committees, strained, breathless, and hurried, panting through a never-ending programme of appointments. We are too busy to be good wives to our husbands, good homemakers, good companions of our children, good friends to our friends, and with no time at all to be friends to the friendless.
>
> But if we withdraw from public engagements and interests, in order to spend quiet hours with the family, the guilty calls of citizenship whisper disquieting claims in our ears. Our children's schools should receive our interest, the civic problems of our community need our attention, the wider issues of the nation and of the world are heavy upon us. Our professional status, our social obligations, our membership in this or that very important organisation, put claims on us. And in our frantic fidelity we try to meet at least the necessary minimum of calls upon us.

But we're weary and breathless. And we know and regret that our life is slipping away, with our having tasted so little of the peace and joy and serenity we are persuaded it should yield to a soul of wide calibre.

If that is all too frequently our condition, what hope is born within us when we see the man perfectly filled with the Spirit, a man who knew excruciating pressure upon him, moving with serenity of spirit from task to task? What was his secret? What can we glean for ourselves who are but beginners in the life of the Spirit?

His secret was a supernatural one. His serenity was such that no worldling could possess. He who could say, 'Peace is my parting gift to you, my own peace, such as the world cannot give. Set your troubled hearts at rest, and banish your fears' (John 14:27) had himself experienced that fruit of the Spirit, that divine gift of God to his children, that blessing 'which is beyond our utmost understanding': the peace of God. And the peace of God had kept guard over his heart and his thoughts (see Philippians 4:7).

It *is* possible for our hearts and thoughts to be so guarded by the peace of God that we are enabled to live a life of inner serenity, however active our hands may be called to be or whatever the pressures that may be brought to bear on us. A few have attained it as a virtually permanent state of mind, some have reached it intermittently, most perhaps only fleetingly. But he who has known this peace, however briefly, is forever haunted by its beauty and his soul cannot rest until it rests in God.

This miraculous peace of God which passes human understanding is part of the Spirit's ministry to the human soul, and in the measure that we learn to open ourselves to that Spirit and entrust our affairs to him, so an amazing simplification of our lives will follow. There will be time and energy for the essentials, and courage to say no to the rest. And all around us, above us, beneath us, and within us will be an unfathomable and inexpressible peace.

9

A remarkably God-dependent man

WE have noted that the Man perfectly filled with the Spirit led an extremely active life and yet was able to retain an inner serenity despite the pressures. Our study would be incomplete without a comment on the perfect balance which he achieved between the contemplative and active life. It has been well said that the man who prays much but gives little in service is like the Dead Sea, which because it lies below sea level, only receives from the rivers flowing into it. It never gives, and has therefore become salty and lifeless. Conversely, the man who serves much and prays little is like the desert pool which quickly dries out in the heat of the sun. But the man who has learnt to find the balance between receiving and giving is like the Sea of Galilee, which receives in abundance from the mountain streams, but also gives in abundance, and whose waters therefore remain crystal clear, fresh and life-giving.

The Man perfectly filled with the Spirit was only able to maintain a ministry to others in which there was a sustained outflowing of spiritual power, because at the same time he was receiving a sustained inpouring of spiritual resources. Jesus lived the truly balanced life—activity balanced by passivity, output by intake.

But this balance has not always been achieved by his followers. There is something slightly nauseating about the hyper-spiritual person who, to the exclusion of all else, nurses obsessively his 'spiritual experience' with all the anxious concern of a hypochondriac—but who never lets his religion overflow in a concern for others. And yet there is also something very sad in the sight of obviously dedicated people frantically seeking to 'do their duty' to God by a ceaseless round of activity, when often the inner well which alone gives meaning to the activity has long since run dry.

They are like people who continue to write and hand out cheques though they have nothing left in the bank.

How did Jesus ensure that there were always sufficient funds in his spiritual bank account? These glimpses from the gospels give us the clue: 'Very early next morning he got up and went out. He went away to a lonely spot and remained there in prayer' (Mark 1:35). 'After taking leave of them, he went up the hillside to pray' (Mark 6:46). 'And from time to time he would withdraw to lonely places for prayer' (Luke 5:16). 'During this time he went out one day into the hills to pray, and spent the night in prayer to God' (Luke 6:12).

The Man perfectly filled with the Spirit knew the secret of withdrawing 'from time to time' in order to replenish through prayer that which had been expended. It was a secret his disciples wanted to learn. 'Lord, teach us to pray, as John taught his disciples,' they said to him (Luke 11:1). It is a secret we all need to learn.

There is probably no other factor of the spiritual life which produces a more widespread inferiority complex among Christians than the subject of private prayer. Though convinced of its importance, many have to admit that their various attempts at establishing a regular, disciplined and programmed devotional life have proved hard going. And in settling for something less arduous they have ended up with a feeling of failure, defeat and guilt. But we can be quite sure that Jesus never meant prayer to be associated with a feeling of failure, and it could be that the sense of guilt is misplaced. It could arise from something as simple as not giving due recognition to the differences that exist in both natural and Spirit-given capacity for prayer.

Some people have a natural talent for prayer. Prayer in its very simplest forms—the cry for help, the sense of awe, the exclamation of joy—is an instinctive tendency, a gift shared by all. But as with all other gifts, it is not given in equal measure to all. The capacity for sustained mental prayer varies tremendously from person to person. The church is made up of Marthas as well as Marys. And it is no reflection on Peter to say that John probably had the greater temperamental affinity for prayer. There is a variety of natural gifts, and a natural talent for prayer is not given to everyone. Each person needs therefore to find his own level in prayer. He needs to develop the capacity granted him, but without letting those more generously endowed make him feel inferior. It is unfortunate that so much formal teaching on prayer reflects the experience of geniuses of the spiritual life, and that the idea has spread that what is right for the genius is a must for every believer. It is as if Beethoven had decreed that enjoying a good tune was not enough and that a true appreciation of music could only be gained through a mastery of Bach's contrapuntal technique. And it must be added that even for those exceptionally gifted much current teaching on techniques of prayer seems to stand in startling contrast with the simplicity of the teaching Jesus gave to his disciples, and the natural spontaneity of his own praying.

But not only are there differences in natural talent for prayer. Feelings of inadequacy can mistakenly arise when we fail to recognise that to some is given a special 'gift of prayer' through their experience of the Holy Spirit. Prayer 'takes off' for them. What has previously seemed like a discipline becomes a delight. Communion with God is established at a deeper level than ever before. And hearing them speak of their new-found spontaneity in prayer makes every heart yearn to share their experience. But it is the result of a gift, a gift granted by the Spirit. And the gifts of the Spirit are not at our command. We must therefore learn to rejoice with those who rejoice and to reject any temptation to despise our own, different, but equally valid gifts.

The life of prayer has been likened to trying to push-start a car. The effort is made with the hope that the engine will quickly fire—and from then everything will be easy. Some people seem only to have pushed their prayer car five feet when 'something happens', and they are off and away for long stretches at a time. For other, equally sincere, believers the story is different. After pushing their prayer car with disciplined effort for what seems like many blocks, the engine splutters into life and the car roars away—but only to stop again a moment later. And then it is back to pushing again until the next rewarding sign of life. For these Christians prayer remains a discipline, a slow advance marked by the occasional moment of sensed illumination. And the joyful testimonies of those who (seemingly effortlessly) soar past can in these circumstances have a negative rather than a positive effect. But the value of prayer in replenishing inner resources cannot be measured by our feelings, and even he who frequently has to get out and push can take comfort from the fact that he too is advancing along the way.

It is precisely because 'the gifts we possess differ as they are allotted to us by God's grace' (Romans 12:6), and because there are such differences in both natural and Spirit-given capacity for prayer, that each of us in his own way must seek to discover the secret of drawing on those hidden resources which alone enabled the Man perfectly filled with the Spirit to live the truly balanced life. 'Come with me, by yourselves, to some lonely place where you can rest quietly' (Mark 6:31) was what our Lord said to his disciples after an exceptionally busy period. It is still his word to us today.

10

A remarkably caring man

'IT was a heaven of love that came into my heart,' wrote Samuel Brengle of his infilling by the Holy Spirit. 'I walked out over Boston Common before breakfast, weeping for joy and praising God. Oh, how I loved! In that hour I knew Jesus, and I loved him till it seemed my heart would break with love. I loved the sparrows, I loved the dogs, I loved the horses, I loved the little urchins on the streets, I loved the strangers who hurried past me, I loved the heathen—I loved the whole world.' Paul exulted in the same experience. 'God has poured out his love into our hearts', he wrote to the Christians in Rome, 'by means of the Holy Spirit, who is God's gift to us' (Romans 5:5, *Good News Bible*).

But there is nothing surprising in this. For if the very essence of God is love, it follows that the very essence of the Holy Spirit also is love, and that when we open ourselves to an inpouring of that Spirit the essence of that experience will be love. The graphic words of a recent testimony could not describe it more beautifully: 'It was as if liquid love was being poured into the entire depths of my soul.' We must not be tempted to think that that is a poetic way of referring to a generally benevolent attitude of goodwill towards mankind, as might animate a citizens' group to put up a new playground. What we are talking about here is an invasion of the personality by a new emotion, a supernatural quality which, in the testimony of those who have known the experience to a powerful degree, is utterly beyond anything they have previously known. The soul yearns for God, for the natural world, yearns for mankind. It even yearns for its enemies. And though the blazing intensity of the emotional experience may eventually subside, the supernatural flame of love for God and concern for others remains alight.

John did not hesitate to make the possession of this supernatural quality an objective test of whether a person was truly God-indwelt or not. 'Everyone who loves is a child of God', he writes, 'and knows God, but the unloving know nothing of God. . . . God is love; he who dwells in love is dwelling in God, and God in him' (1 John 4:7, 8, 16). Albert Orsborn expresses a similar thought in his classic couplet:

Except I am moved with compassion,
How dwelleth thy Spirit in me?

Now if souls with limited capacity for receiving have been so deeply moved with compassion through an experience of the Spirit, how much more would we expect to find this to be the very heart of the divine infilling which the man with unlimited capacity to receive experienced at the River Jordan. That it was so is beyond the shadow of a doubt. We have no record of Jesus describing his emotion as 'liquid love' or anything else—but his life is his testimony, and all the more eloquent for that. Impulsed by the Spirit of love that burnt within him, he gave himself so utterly and so effectively to meeting the needs of his contemporaries that 'their astonishment knew no bounds: "All that he does, he does well," they said' (Mark 7:37). In him the love of God, invisible before, became visible. He cared for his brothers and sisters, 'his heart went out to them, because they were like sheep without a shepherd' (Mark 6:34), and they sensed it, and sought him out everywhere to share with him their woes and problems.

Two points that may enable us to understand our own experience better in the light of his. His love was focused. It was not an abstract love for the world in general, but a focused compassion that expressed itself to real people and in real, concrete details. He loved his disciples—and spent hours with them, teaching them and sharing with them. He loved the man with the paralysed hand—and healed him. He loved the crowd that had come from afar to hear him—and he taught them until sunset. He loved the man in the grip of an evil spirit—and set him free. He loved the social outcasts—and invited them for a meal. He did not need to go around announcing that he loved the world. People knew it. Through him they felt focused upon themselves the infinite love of God.

Spirit-impulsed caring is always focused. My father-in-law, Brigadier Thomas Turner, a corps officer for over 30 years, was a man seemingly uniquely linked with his flocks past and present by bonds of love and affection. In him I saw a new meaning to focused caring. The stories of how he would be late for dinner because 'old Mrs Smith's garden fence had fallen down in the storm and I had to stay to fix it', became part of family lore. Where there was a need he got down to trying to meet it, whether it was decorating a room, doing the garden, seeing the solicitor for someone, or spending hour after hour in patient counselling.

I well remember arriving with my wife at the parental home to find every conceivable corner of it occupied by hyacinths planted in individual pots. Under the stairs, behind the settee, on the landing—everywhere, hyacinths. 'I am growing these for the over-60 club,' he explained. 'At Christmas every member will receive one.' Focused loving. In themselves small things, but to the recipient the tangible evidence of divine caring. Is it surprising that up and down the British Isles he is remembered with almost astonishing affection?

Second, the love of Jesus was unlimited. 'Love your enemies,' he said. 'If you love only those who love you, what reward can you expect? Surely the tax-gatherers do as much as that' (Matthew 5:44, 46). He showed by his life what it means to love even when our love is spurned. But how easy it is to confine our own caring only to those who reciprocate, or at least appreciate, our love.

That outstanding Salvation Army missionary, Ruth Siegfried, tells of a time when her love was tested to the limit. She had given her life to the building up of an educational programme in the Congo, had toiled and sacrificed everything, including health and strength, so that her beloved African young people could receive an education. Her reward was not so much the imposing building that had been erected as the alert, lively young people who were advancing in knowledge under her tuition.

But one day the blow fell. There was a delegation of teenagers outside her door. Shuffling their feet, obviously embarrassed, their spokesman finally blurted out their request. 'We want you to go, major,' they said. She had given them all the knowledge she had, they explained, and unless she went away no one with greater qualifications who could take them further would be sent. The inner turmoil was traumatic. After a life devoted to their welfare—this! But she knew they were right. She loved them to the limit—and beyond. She went.

11

A remarkably fearless man

IT is a thousand pities that the word child rhymes with mild, for that, as Leslie Weatherhead has pointed out, has given us the lines:

Gentle Jesus, meek and mild,
Look upon a little child.

A gentle Jesus, yes. Even a meek Jesus, in the full sense of that term. But a mild Jesus, never. What stood out about him was his strength, his boldness, his fearlessness. Single-handed he was challenging the established order. By the third chapter of Mark's gospel the authorities are already plotting how to get rid of him. To take a whip and by force eject the money-changers from the Temple is not the action of a mild man, and when Peter and John were later to stand accused before the same authorities that had crucified their Master they were recognised as having been with Jesus not by their gentleness, their meekness or their mildness. It was 'when they saw the fearlessness of Peter and John . . . they recognised them as having been among the supporters of Jesus' (Acts 4:13, *Barclay*).

Jesus was brought up on the law and tradition and regarded them with great respect. But religious structures, however good and God-given, tend to become rigid, and through the life-giving Spirit within him he saw that the religion of his day had become mostly outward observance. He longed to open new windows for his people, to show them God was more than a law-giver; he was Spirit, 'and those who worship him must worship in spirit and in truth' (John 4:24).

But this could not be achieved without challenging some of the traditions with which the law had become encrusted—and that put him on a direct collision course with the religious leaders of his day.

And it was not only 'the Jews' that 'murmured disapprovingly'. 'Many of his disciples on hearing it exclaimed, "This is more than we can stomach! Why listen to such talk?" . . . From that time on, many of his disciples withdrew and no longer went about with him' (John 6:60 and 66). It takes a special kind of courage to continue with one's ministry when there is opposition not only from without but also from within.

The natural instinct of man is to go with the herd, to be carried by the stream, to conform. But the man who opens himself to the Spirit of God often finds himself impulsed in the opposite direction to that in which the world, and sometimes seemingly his fellow Christians, are going. And like someone trying to make his way against the stream of rush-hour traffic he stands and gets honked at. Some shrink from it and find the Spirit quenched within them. Others, not without trepidation, seek to follow in the footsteps of the Man perfectly filled with the Spirit, and take comfort in the thought that courage is not the absence of fear but the conquest of fear.

Opposition from within the group is often more difficult to cope with than opposition from without. We are braced for that. It is not only in the army barrack room that the fear of being labelled a 'holy Joe' has deterred a young man from responding to the inner whisper calling him to adventure in the Spirit. The devil knows his way equally well to the Salvation Army bandroom. An innocent crack can make the sensitive soul shut tight like a clam. Someone has remarked, the spiritual temperature in the average church is so low that when someone comes along whose temperature is normal, everyone thinks he has a fever! 'And you wouldn't want them to think that,' cautions the tempter, and the damage is done.

When Herbert Booth penned the lines 'From all the care of what men think or say, cleansing for me,' he was probably not thinking of the group pressure from within the Christian circle. But it exists. Ask anyone who has attended youth councils. And he who would be like his Master must summon the courage to resist that pressure, or his life will be shaped not by the Spirit but by the group. Jesus aroused such intense opposition because he felt called to break the hardened clay of the religious structure of his day. And no area is of greater sensitivity, for human nature clings grimly and protectively to its religious traditions however empty they might become.

Many people who have been awakened to new spiritual reality through an experience of the Spirit become intensely aware of the shortcomings of the particular Christian tradition in which they have been nurtured, and become filled with reforming zeal. They should not be surprised by the degree of protective hostility they frequently encounter. We must not close our eyes to the fact that religious structures, unless continually renewed, tend to ossify and imprison those within, and The Salvation Army cannot expect to be exempt from this tendency.

The Salvation Army began in an explosion of Holy Spirit power. The early salvationists rejoiced in the glorious liberty of the sons of God, and defying all opposition prided themselves on their innovative and creative nonconformity. But the nonconformist of yesterday has a tendency to become the conformist of today and the reactionary of tomorrow. And the movement which becomes obsessively bent on preserving intact and unchanged that which was created of old by the Spirit, risks being left behind by that Spirit, for the Spirit is always young, always free, always new. No church can therefore afford to kill off its prophets.

But for the man who would dare, in the name of the Spirit, to challenge the cherished values of his colleagues, fearlessness is not enough. He needs divine wisdom too, for fearlessness and foolishness make a fatal combination. Foolishness forgets that the work of the Holy Spirit is always consistent and continuous, and that he does not suddenly reject today what he himself created yesterday. And The Salvation Army was born of the Spirit and in the Spirit it was nurtured. But sometimes those who have been awakened spiritually through the influence of some other Christian tradition feel that the values, customs and even doctrines of that tradition are the only ones through which the Spirit can work, and they forget that the Army too, in all its uniqueness, is a creation of the Spirit. Too often they want to reject what the Spirit wants to renew.

It is only with the 'wisdom from above' which is 'peace-loving, considerate, and open to reason' (James 3:17) that true renewal can take place. What the Army needs are prophets clad in red jerseys gifted with that wisdom.

12

A remarkably unpretentious man

WHEN Charles Dickens created the grovelling character of Uriah Heep, with his 'I am so very 'umble, Master Copperfield; so very 'umble,' he compounded the already very great difficulties of commenting meaningfully on that gracious character trait which the *Authorised Version* calls meekness, the *New English Bible* gentleness, and the *Good News Bible* humility (Galatians 5:22). For Uriah Heep symbolises the deep-seated suspicion of humbug, inverted pride, of a hidden inferiority complex, or simply a lack of drive with which humility is often viewed.

To Caiaphas and the other religious and social leaders, Jesus was the Che Guevara of the first century. A dangerous and fearless revolutionary leader. But whereas it would strain one's credulity to believe that Che's strong personality included meekness, gentleness and humility among its qualities, it is another indication of the greatness of Jesus that within the one personality he could combine ruggedness with tenderness, strength with gentleness and confidence with humility.

When Jesus took the bowl of water and the towel and began to wash the disciples' feet he was engaging in symbolism but he was not putting on an act. You can't fool a group of people you have been living with for three years. No doubt the painful memory was still vivid in their minds of the time when they had become jealous of the Zebedee brothers' request for special prominence in the Kingdom, and he had made use of the occasion to tell them: 'Among you, whoever wants to be great must be your servant, and whoever wants to be first must be the willing slave of all—like the Son of Man; he did not come to be served, but to serve' (Matthew 20:26-28). And watching him washing their feet they had to admit that many times he had seemed just that—the willing slave of all.

This quality of meekness, gentleness, humility, is a shimmering quality that vanishes when you touch it in order to examine it. Paul spoke about love never being 'boastful, nor conceited, nor rude' (1 Corinthians 13:4) and exhorted the Romans to 'not be conceited or think too highly of yourself; but think your way to a sober estimate based on the measure of faith that God has dealt to each of you' (Romans 12:3). But the quality defies precise definition. And this fruit of the Spirit cannot be force-grown in a spiritual hot-house. It is the indirect and spontaneous outcome of the soul's openness to the Spirit. No man can ever claim to possess it without forfeiting it. Even the old joke about the new convert testifying to being proud of his humility comes too close to being true to life to be comfortable.

About the only thing one can do is to observe this quality in the lives of those who are truly God-indwelt and pray that 'the beauty of Jesus' might also be seen in us.

Take Jean-Marie Vianney, the curé d'Ars, for instance. William Sangster tells in *The Pure in Heart* of how when Vianney arrived in Ars the village had sunk very low. 'Sunday was desecrated: the cabarets and dance-halls were full: ignorance was widespread, blasphemy, impurity and lying were features of that rural life.' The curé set to work to remedy this but aroused intense opposition. For 10 years 'this obscure village was the scene of a major contest of hell and heaven'. Slanderous stories began circulating about him. He was accused of attracting girls to his house for immoral purposes. 'His pale face and wasted frame—the fruit of fastings and midnight prayers—were offered as evidence of his evil living. He was the subject of obscene songs and scurrilous anonymous letters. A woman of the street paraded under his window night after night, accusing him in filthy phrases to all the neighbourhood of being the father of her child. When he came down in the morning, it was often to find his door encrusted with the refuse his accusers and their dupes had flung at it in the night.'

But the opposition was not only from without. His fellow-clerics in the diocese were openly hostile. 'Aware of his lack of learning, they wrote him letters saying that he disgraced the cloth, and that it was in their mind to petition the bishops to have him removed, and he replied to all but the anonymous ones with gratitude, begging the prayers of his correspondents that "I may do less harm and more good".' They did in the end prepare a petition and, when it was ready and signed, one of the priests 'either from bravado or remorse' sent it to the curé d'Ars himself. He studied it carefully, and tearfully agreed with all that it said about his ignorance and incompetence. 'When it arrived on the bishop's desk, his own signature had been appended also.'

Meek, gentle, humble—the curé d'Ars shared his Master's qualities, and through his indomitable faith eventually won through. The time came when cabarets and dance halls folded up: when foul language was heard in Ars no more: when the church was crowded with eager worshippers. 'It is not that we are better than other people,' explained a resident to a visitor from Paris, 'but there are things you cannot do when there is a saint about.'

The qualities of meekness and humility also shine in less heroic circumstances than Ars. For example, it is impossible to think of that outstandingly gifted Salvation Army leader, General Frederick Coutts, without these qualities coming to mind. And yet, somehow, the words do not seem quite right to describe the General. It is not only that each has gathered to itself a cluster of pejorative associations, it is that, somehow they seem altogether too pretentious, for it is the very unpretentiousness of the man that stands out. *Unpretentiousness?* Have we by a round-about route arrived at yet another translation of that untranslatable quality which the Greeks called *praotes*?

The stories in circulation about the General's unassuming ways are legion—from the sight of him popping out from International Headquarters and returning with a loaf under his arm, in readiness for the meal he would later be preparing for his sick wife, to his role in retirement as corps pianist of St Albans Corps. It is in the sum of such glimpses taken from everyday life that the true measure of the man is to be seen.

On arriving in London to assume the Generalship, General and Mrs Coutts had their soldiership transferred to the small corps of South Croydon, in whose district they lived. After a few months, when the first gap appeared in the General's busy programme of congresses around the world, with their vast crowds, television appearances, press conferences and interviews with national leaders, he was due to visit his own corps where he had agreed to conduct the meetings.

The divisional commander who tells the story decided he had better be there in good time for the 10 am open-air meeting lest the General should decide to turn up. The divisional commander arrived at 10 to 10, found the hall open but nobody around. He waited until 10, and then in the company of another comrade who had arrived set out for the designated venue. Approaching the street they could hear the small band playing, and rounding the corner they saw the open-air meeting in progress. The lieutenant with his cornet was leading his usual group of five players. But today there was a sixth. The General was playing the E*b* bass!

We must be unpretentious servants of an unpretentious Master.

13

A remarkably radical man

'WHY this waste?' was the reaction of some who sat at table with Jesus when Mary broke the bottle of costly perfume and poured it over our Lord's head. 'They turned upon her with fury,' records Mark (14:5). But Jesus sprang to her defence. He understood love's extravagance, the desire to give beyond what prudence would dictate. He himself by nature found it difficult to do things by halves. With him it was all or nothing. 'Let her alone,' replied Jesus with a touch of asperity in his voice. 'Why must you make trouble for her? It is a fine thing she has done for me' (Mark 14:6).

Jesus had a well-developed radical streak in his personality. He was extreme in what he expected from his followers—and in what he was prepared to give himself. 'You must not think that I have come to bring peace to the earth,' he said bluntly. 'I have not come to bring peace, but a sword. I have come to set a man against his father, a daughter against her mother. . . . No man is worthy of me who does not take up his cross and walk in my footsteps. By gaining his life a man will lose it; by losing his life for my sake, he will gain it' (Matthew 10:34, 35, 38, 39).

Religion has been called the opium of the people, an expression that conjures up the picture of it keeping the masses contented and docile while lulling their sensibilities. It has also been thought of as a veneer of respectability, its norms and practices providing a skin-deep façade of decent behaviour that enables society to function smoothly. But nothing could be farther from the truth. Outward religious observance may have that effect, but opening oneself to the Spirit of God is anything but like lulling oneself with a sweet drug or being coated with a varnish.

It is like touching a live high tension wire. The impact has been known to shatter and remake the personality in an instant, and has impelled countless souls to a degree of self-giving they would previously not have thought possible. Moderation is thrown to the wind and previously carefully calculated service for God becomes a spontaneous, almost reckless, outpouring of the self which to the onlooker is utterly incomprehensible.

'Why this waste?' they said of Stephen as the stones were flung at him, stunning him to death as the first Christian martyr. 'If only he had tempered his words a bit none of this would have happened.'

'Why this waste?' they said of Father Damian, as he set out to give his life to a handful of lepers in a distant island.

'Why this waste?' they said of the brilliant Henry Martyn when, discarding the many careers open to him, he set sail for India in response to the Lord's call.

'Why this waste?' they said of Samuel Brengle when he allied himself to the despised Salvation Army. 'With his eloquence his future was assured within the Church.'

'Why this waste?' they said of Albert Schweitzer, doctor of music and doctor of theology, when he abandoned all that and, having trained as a doctor of medicine, went and 'buried himself' in Africa.

'Why this waste?' they are saying of the young Russian who is serving a long sentence in a labour camp for being unemployed, when a small adjustment to his faith, a mere technical denial, would have secured him the work permit he needed to gain employment.

The world will never understand self-giving and sacrifice of heroic proportions, and neither will everyone within the Church. But the Man perfectly filled with the Spirit understood, for he too felt the compulsion of that same Spirit leading him to a total abandonment of himself to the will of his Father.

'Why this waste?' they must have said of him as he hung on the cross. 'Such a good man, such talent, such promise. Of course, he went too far. And now look at him!'

But reckless self-giving, when rightly directed, releases energy for good that is incalculable in its results.

Where a number of such like-spirited believers band together the Church becomes invincible. Spurning moderation as well as opposition, persecution and death, the 120 of Pentecost were quickly to rock the foundations of the Roman Empire. 'We must obey God rather than men,' was their motto. In an unintended compliment, the mob in Thessalonica complained that they who had 'turned the world upside down' had come there also.

The Salvation Army's early history reflects something of this same explosive force. With complete disregard for personal comfort, reputation and safety, and frequently against strong opposition, its officers turned communities upside down and challenged the social evils of the day. That the Army's Chief of the Staff was put on trial at the Old Bailey is evidence of the lengths to which the movement was prepared to go.

These lines are being written in South America, where for centuries the Church has been linked with the established forces within society. One could depend on the Church to play for safety, to support the *status quo* and be against progress. But of recent years the wind of change—the wind of the Holy Spirit—has swept over the Church and the effect has been startling. Its leaders have regained something of the apostolic vision, power and courage, and the Church has become the great disturber of the established order, questioning, cajoling, prodding and pushing reactionary rulers into social reform—sometimes at great personal risk to the leaders involved. Not everyone would agree with every method employed, but there is no denying the new dynamism of the Church.

The high voltage current of power flowed unimpeded through the man Jesus, that perfect conductor of the Spirit, and made him a radical for God. Not only was his self-giving total, but he was prepared to go to the ultimate length to obey God rather than men. Not all of his followers have been prepared to be like him in that respect. The fear of God, in the sense of being afraid of what the Spirit might lead us into, is a very real thing—and effectively blocks the Spirit from being released within us.

The Holy Spirit needs no 'Danger—High Tension' warning sign, for human nature knows intuitively the risks involved. And many simply do not want to be turned inside out in order to turn the world upside down. They prefer to leave such heroics to others. With their lips they may be imploring the Spirit to take control, but deep down where it counts the heart is holding the door firmly shut.

14

A remarkably long-suffering man

IT was Evelyn Underhill who with deep insight remarked that suffering plunges like a sword through humanity, leaving on the one side cringing and degraded creatures and on the other heroes and saints. One of life's great mysteries is why some people have to suffer so much. For them calamity succeeds calamity in a seemingly never-ending chain. But even those whom life has favoured will experience their points of crisis, for suffering is the common lot of mankind, and whether a man becomes stunted or grows through such an experience depends on how he reacts to it. It is the set of the sail that determines whether the storm wind drives the ship onwards or to disaster. Whether it be the blast of failure, doubt, humiliation, loneliness, frustration, hardship, fading powers, thwarted ambition, sorrow, ill health, spiritual darkness, unreturned love or love that cannot be expressed—it is how we set out to sail that counts. It is at the point of crisis that we see the true man.

The supreme crisis point for Jesus, the Man perfectly filled with the Spirit, came near the end of his ministry. In anguish of spirit he retired to the garden of Gethsemane to pray. He knew what the ultimate outcome would be if he persisted in his course, but this was more than a choice between living or dying. The hideous spectre of doubt must have been leering at him. Had it all been a huge mistake? There, too, was the excruciating pain of rejected love. His mental anguish was such that 'his sweat was like clots of blood falling to the ground' (Luke 22:44). 'Father, if it be thy will, take this cup away from me,' he prayed in his agony (Luke 22:42). But this plea was immediately followed by that most significant of small words, the word which the *Authorised Version* renders as 'nevertheless'. 'Nevertheless', he said, 'not my will, but thine, be done.' He did not try to hide his longing to escape suffering. Here was no foolhardy rush towards the enemy lines like a soldier seeking immortal glory. None of that morbid desire for suffering which has marred the image of some of the historical saints, and which made St Teresa exclaim: 'Let me suffer or die!' But neither was there a cowardly retreat. If there could be no escape, he would accept his lot, he would face up to suffering. 'Up, let us go forward!' he said to his disciples. 'My betrayer is upon us' (Mark 14:42).

The New Testament word which described this accepting but conquering attitude to the tests of life is quite untranslatable by one single word in English. It is usually rendered as long-suffering or patience, but both these words have overtones of passive resignation and fail to bring out the note of defiance. Our Lord's was a 'conquering patience' (Barclay), a defiant acceptance that turned defeat into victory. Paul, who was no stranger to suffering, spoke of trying to recommend himself by his steadfast endurance in 'all circumstances . . . in distress, hardships, and dire straits; flogged, imprisoned, mobbed; overworked, sleepless, starving' (2 Corinthians 6:4)—and that throws further light on this quality of the Christian character. But to get a phrase that adequately sums up the attitude to suffering of the Man perfectly filled with the Spirit we need to add the word 'triumphing'. His was a steadfast, triumphing endurance.

Things had got on top of a Salvation Army missionary officer serving in India. The incessant demands, the insoluble problems, the hostility of community leaders and the misunderstandings from within her flock had all proved too much. It was decided that she should rest for some weeks in the lovely mountain lodge provided for missionaries in need of refreshment. She tells of arriving at the house dejected and depressed and being shown to her room with its majestic view of the snowclad mountains. But what struck her most was not the view but the words of a framed text that hung on the wall. Its words were to be the words of healing for her. It simply said, 'Not somehow but triumphantly!' During the next weeks those words were to become engraved on her mind. They seemed both to diagnose her condition and show her the way to recovery. She knew that for too long, as each new crisis had come along, she had bowed her head in fatalistic submission and hoped that somehow she would get by, somehow muddle through, somehow keep going until her term of service was up. Even in her own spiritual life 'somehow' had become enough. But the implied promise of the wall-text stirred her dormant faith back into life. 'Not somehow but triumphantly!' With the help of the Holy Spirit those very problems that had bowed her down could become the stepping stones to greater faith, greater trust and greater victories. No longer was it going to be *somehow*. it was going to be *triumphantly!*

Steadfast and triumphing endurance of adversity is a mark of the Spirit-filled man. It is one of the gifts of the Spirit. It is a quality that lies dormant until the hour of need. We may marvel at the fortitude of fellow believers and wonder however we ourselves could cope with their problems, but grace is not given in advance, it becomes ours when we need it. 'He giveth more grace as our burdens grow greater,' wrote Annie Johnson Flint, reflecting the promise of old 'as thy days, so shall thy strength be' (Deuteronomy 33:25, *AV*). We will not be expected to face tomorrow's problems on today's supply of grace.

'My grace' (the strength of my indwelling presence) 'is all you need,' said the risen Lord to Paul when he was racked by suffering, 'power comes to its full strength in weakness' (2 Corinthians 12:9). And the reality of this experience for Paul was such that he could say: 'I shall therefore prefer to find my joy and pride in the very things that are my weakness; and then the power of Christ will come and rest upon me.' He ends with the astonishing assertion, with its—to the ears of the world—almost crazy contrasts: 'Hence I am well content, for Christ's sake, with weakness, contempt, persecution, hardship, and frustration; for when I am weak, then I am strong' (2 Corinthians 12:10).

Talk about steadfast and triumphing endurance! On the one hand cringing and degraded creatures, on the other heroes and saints. But more than that. The man who emerges victorious, however battle-scarred, from the test of suffering is granted a gift precious beyond price: the gift of being able to enter into the profoundest depths of the feelings of those who are passing through suffering—in order to help them reach the other side. He understands the awful horror of the long dark night of suffering, the despair that threatens to engulf, the times when but for some invisible power from above or some deep-seated survival instinct one would have slipped over the edge—and the hand stretched out is gratefully grasped. 'In love's service only wounded soldiers may serve.'

15

A remarkably joyful man

'LOR' bless you, sir,' said the beaming salvationist drummer to Dr Farmer, the scholarly organist at Harrow, who had pleaded with him not to hit the drum so hard, 'Since I've been converted I'm so happy I could bust the bloomin' drum!' That classic cameo deserves an honoured place in The Salvation Army's picture gallery for it captures to perfection one of the chief features of early Army life: the spontaneous, uninhibited, all-pervading joy with which it was suffused. When in his celebrated attack Huxley called the Army 'a manifestation of corybantic Christianity'—a reference to the Corybantes, priests of Cybele, who in their festivals beat cymbals and behaved exuberantly—he thought he was insulting it. But not at all. The salvationists clapped their hands and beat their drums and banged their tambourines and shouted their hallelujahs because they could do no other. They were so happy that there was no way of stopping their emotions from spilling over into action.

No one has put it better than William Pearson:

Joy! joy! joy! there is joy in The Salvation Army,
Joy! joy! joy! in the Army of the Lord.
Sing to God, sing to God, with loud joyful songs of praise;
Beat the drums, beat the drums, while salvation music plays.
Play the music, play, sing the happy song,
Loud hosannas shout with the happy throng,
To the happy land we'll march along,
And be joyful all the way.
Joy! joy! joy! there is joy in The Salvation Army,
Joy! joy! joy! in the Army of the Lord.

It is a historical fact that revivals of religion have invariably been accompanied by an outpouring of exultant joy. The 'vast roarings of superhuman happiness' which the individual seekers frequently experience, overspill into the community until all are caught up in an inextinguishable gladness of heart. And where the inhibitions are few this joy manifests itself in boisterous fashion. The followers of Francis of Assisi came to be called God's gleemen and had to be reproved for laughing in church!

The classical saints were joyous personalities, often despite adversity. Even when Catherine of Siena was prostrate with illness she 'overflowed with gaiety and gladness, and was full of laughter in the Lord, exultant and rejoicing'. And the visionaries have always perceived that joy lies at the heart of all reality. Dante, initiated into Paradise, sees the whole universe laugh with delight as it glorifies God. Tertullian in an early century put it into a nutshell: the Christian saint is hilarious!

When we move into New Testament times this atmosphere of joy becomes even more marked. 'The New Testament,' comments Harry Emerson Fosdick, 'is the most joyful book in the world. It opens with joy over the birth of Jesus; and it ends with a superb picture of a multitude which no man could number, singing hallelujah choruses. No matter where you open it, amid fortunate or discouraging circumstances, you always hear the note of joy.' And Johannes Weis in his monumental *Earliest Christianity* reckoned that 'unless one can understand this constant mood of victorious, jubilant happiness and confidence, one simply will not understand primitive Christianity.'

The New Testament writers had no doubt as to the source of this superabundant joy. The source was the Holy Spirit—the Spirit of joy. 'The kingdom of God is . . . joy, inspired by the Holy Spirit,' wrote Paul (Romans 14:17). And he speaks of exulting in God 'with the joy that comes from the Holy Spirit' (1 Thessalonians 1:6, *Good News Bible*). 'The harvest of the Spirit is . . . joy', he declares in Galatians 5:22. Peter refers to believers being 'transported with a joy too great for words' (1 Peter 1:8) and Luke's final comment on the eventful days Paul and Barnabus spent in Antioch is that 'the converts were filled with joy and with the Holy Spirit' (Acts 13:52).

As we move yet further back into history, it would have been strange indeed if the Man most filled with the Spirit of joy had not himself been an outstandingly happy man. Though we may have to wrench ourselves free from the artists' passion week portrayals of him as a man of sorrows—portrayals which have dominated the popular perception of him—the total picture we get of him from the pages of the gospels makes it clear that he was a singularly joyful personality. No figure of gloom could have drawn children and outcasts and disciples to his company as he did. John's comment about the risen Jesus, that 'when the disciples saw the Lord, they were filled with joy' (John 20:20), describes what must surely have been their reaction many times before. It was always good to see Jesus and always good to be with him.

The note of joy also abounded in his teaching, and it would be hard to believe that some of his acute comments about life—like the man with the beam in his eye—did not draw laughter from his hearers. And it would have been incongruous for a habitually solemn man to say: 'I have spoken thus to you, so that my joy may be in you, and your joy complete' (John 15:11). No, he who was perfectly filled with the Spirit was a radiant man.

This joy which is characteristic of the Spirit-filled man is an extension of the joy which every man experiences—that precious grace which the creator God has granted to all his children. It is that same joy lifted to the nth degree, where it no longer depends on circumstances, moods or external stimuli. It is joy beyond the capacity of the natural man, and in that sense it is a supernatural gift.

Not everyone, however, can experience joy with the same intensity, nor will it reveal itself in the same way in differing personalities. Joy is an emotion and the capacity for emotional experience varies tremendously from person to person. Without loss of its distinctive Spirit-given quality, what for one will be an ecstatic exultation will for another be a quiet satisfaction. And in God's great wind orchestra there is a variety of instruments, and the same wind will produce many different sounds. The man who is by nature of a positive bent will rejoice all the more through the action of the Spirit, and the wit will become wittier and the wisecracker both wiser and funnier. But even he who by nature tends to be melancholy will in his own way experience joy in the deeps of his nature—and may even surprise by the unexpected radiance of his life.

True joy, 'the joy that comes from the Holy Spirit', comes always from within and cannot be worked up from without. The man who pursues the pleasure of the world, just as much as the meeting leader who tries to dragoon his apathetic congregation to sing and to clap and to beat their tambourines and to smile, is approaching the matter from the wrong end. The result has all the attractiveness of an artificial fruit in the fruit bowl of the Spirit.

But when joy springs from the heart, that is the time to watch out, for the joy of the Lord has been known to make a man want to 'bust the bloomin' drum!'

16

A remarkably steadfast man

THE fruit of the Spirit is reliability. A Christian is faithful, steady, trustworthy, dependable. 'No one who sets his hand to the plough and then keeps looking back is fit for the kingdom of God,' says the Man perfectly filled with the Spirit (Luke 9:62), and he himself exemplified fidelity in the course of his life. When everyone else had looked behind, had abandoned their call, he went on, a solitary rock-like figure. Set in his purpose, determined to see it through, he knew desolation but never looked back.

It is unfortunate that frequently those who have claimed most to be filled with the Spirit have least displayed this quality of determined reliability. With their ups and downs, ins and outs, hot and cold, all go or no go, the Spirit himself has been brought into disrepute, making him appear a Spirit of unreliability, unpredictability, inconsistency and disorder. Evelyn Underhill's trenchant description of Madam Guyon's first fumbling attempts at living in the Spirit could be applied to many. 'The wind that bloweth where it listeth whistled through her soul: and the response which she made was that of a weathercock rather than a windmill. She moved to every current; she often mistook a draught for the divine breath; she felt her gyrations to be of enormous importance.'

The fundamental mistake which many make is to root their spiritual life in their emotions instead of in the will, the true centre of religious life. If instead of concentrating on their fluctuating feelings they would fix their attention on the will, they would be surprised how quickly their emotions would come into line. A spiritual life lived in the emotions is bound to be erratic. What C. S. Lewis called the law of undulation is common to everyone's experience. Our interests, affections, appetites fluctuate; there are ups and downs, there are peaks and troughs, and 'periods of emotional and bodily richness and liveliness alternate with periods of numbness and poverty'. These 'bio-rhythms' are a natural phenomenon that enables the body, mind and soul to recoup their powers after periods of intensity. No one can live at the peak all the time. But woe to him who has tied his faith to his feelings. For the moment those feelings come plunging earthwards in the natural downward circle, down they pull his faith as well. And he who yesterday was jumping to his feet to give a glowing testimony to glory in his soul is today plunged into despair and wrings his hands because he has lost his faith. Fortunately tomorrow's upswing in the bio-rhythms will restore his faith again—until the cycle begins once more.

But these 'yo-yo Christians' give life in the Spirit a bad name, especially where individuals have a natural capacity for intense feeling that enables them to rise to high emotional peaks, for by some immutable law of nature the troughs are correspondingly deep as well. 'We may not experience what he experiences,' say other believers, nodding their heads soberly, 'but at least we are always here for the 10 am open-air meeting.' But where faith is tied to the will, the feelings may rise and fall and come and go, but faith remains constant. There is, in fact, no reason why faith should not remain high even when there are no feelings. It is by faith, not their feelings, that the just shall live. We have been called to be men and women of faith—not of feelings. Periods of spiritual aridity, when feelings dry up, and prayer, the Scriptures, testimony and Christian worship, fellowship and service seem to lose all meaning, are an inescapable part of the Christian walk. Every believer has known those times, and for some they have lasted months, even years.

David Brainerd, that saintly apostle to the North American Indians, pours into his diary his feelings of loneliness and grief at what appears to be his lack of success. 'But what makes all my difficulties grievous to be borne,' he confesses, 'is that *God hides his face from me.*' There is only one way through at these times. The secret is summed up in a blunt way in Richard Slater's old song:

In the fight, say, does your heart grow weary?
Do you find your path is rough and thorny,
And above the sky is dark and stormy?
Never mind, go on!

There really is no other way. Affirming his faith in the Spirit whose fruit is steadfastness, the pilgrim contemplates the sun that has gone out, and the darkness around him, and the numbness of feeling, and the lack of spontaneous interest in things spiritual—and then he straightens his back, says 'never mind' and simply *goes on.* And unlike the hypocrites of whom Jesus spoke, who looked gloomy and made their faces unsightly, he obeys the words of Jesus to 'anoint your head and wash your face, so that men may not see that you are fasting, but only your Father who is in the secret place' (Matthew 6:17, 18).

These periods of dryness are not negative. On the contrary, they make a positive contribution to our growth. God uses these times to teach us to stand on our own feet spiritually. When the new convert is bathed in warm feelings he is like a child learning to walk who is being held tightly by his father. When those feelings are withdrawn he experiences the moment of panic that every child knows when his father lets go, but that 'letting go' is the key to further progress. We only learnt to walk because someone let go of us. We only learn to walk in the Spirit by faith and not feelings when God 'lets go of us'. The periods of dryness are therefore potentially periods of great spiritual progress.

When I was asked to write the music for the sessional song 'Soldiers of Christ' it was the first major work I had attempted. I took it with me on holiday and, to my surprise, within a few days it lay ready—except for a middle section of five lines, twice repeated. There inspiration dried up. I approached it from all angles, but nothing would come. Knowing that the deadline for the song was the end of the holiday I set aside every morning to battle with those five lines at the piano. I played through every sessional song that had previously been written, played the classics, played oratorios, played the tune book, played everything high, middle or low-brow I could lay my hands on in search of a breakthrough. But the heavens were as brass. I can distinctly remember, however, when returning from the village one afternoon, the warmth and delight of the moment when, seemingly miraculously, the missing section unfolded itself to my mind. In its own small way it was a moment of ecstasy, and I can still recapture the glow in memory. But what made me a better musician was not that moment of inspiration, however heart-warming. It was the hours of application and drudgery, the hours of never minding and simply going on that made me grow musically. It is in the troughs and not on the peaks that true progress is made.

'Do not be deceived, Wormwood,' says the senior devil to his junior partner in C. S. Lewis's *The Screwtape Letters.* 'Our cause is never more in danger than when a human, no longer desiring, but still intending, to do our Enemy's will, looks round upon a universe from which every trace of him seems to have vanished, and asks why he has been forsaken, and still obeys.'

17

A remarkably magnanimous man

A REPORTER sent down from outer space to do a piece on some local Christian community might be forgiven if he concluded that the fruit of the Spirit was intolerance, unkindness, meanness, envy, bigotry, prejudice, backbiting, grudge bearing, resentment, negativism, jealousy, narrowness, bitterness, touchiness, pettiness, cussedness and suspicion. A gross exaggeration? Of course it is, but the point to be considered is sufficiently important for a touch of hyperbole to be allowed. For it is a sad fact of Christian life that all too often a spirit of smallness prevails where one would expect to find largeness of mind and soul, and a spirit of magnanimous generosity. Lift the lid off the average Christian group, turn the stone and the creepy-crawlies mentioned above stir into life.

They marred the disciples' band. Said John to Jesus: 'Master, we saw a man driving out devils in your name, and as he was not one of us, we tried to stop him' (Mark 9:38)—a remark that has all the hallmarks of incipient bureaucracy. 'That hasn't gone through the proper channels. It isn't official. Who gave him a commission? Can't have people taking liberties like that!'

It has the marks of exclusivism. 'He isn't one of us. You didn't choose him like you chose us. Who does he think he is?'

It has the marks of suspicion. 'He's an outsider. We don't know what he's like. This thing has got to be controlled. His doctrine could be unsound!'

But the Man perfectly filled with the Spirit would have none of that. He knew his disciples only too well. 'Do not stop him,' said Jesus. . . . 'For he who is not against us is on our side' (Mark 9:39). One of the supreme qualities of that most God-indwelt man, Jesus of Nazareth, was his magnanimity, his generosity of spirit. 'No injuries could embitter and no antipathies could narrow his soul.' There was no trace of meanness in him. And he lived what he taught. Brothers who went on wronging one another were to be forgiven 70 times seven. Enemies were to be loved. 'Do good to those who hate you,' he said. 'Bless those who curse you; pray for those who treat you spitefully' (Luke 6:28).

The Man perfectly filled with the Spirit was 'patient, kind and envied no one', to adapt Paul's great love portrait of him in 1 Corinthians 13:4-6. He was 'never boastful, nor conceited, nor rude; never selfish, not quick to take offence.' He kept no score of wrongs, did not gloat over other men's sins, but delighted in the truth. He was 'always eager to believe the best' (verse 7, *Moffatt*). He was magnanimity personified. His was a big heart and a big mind and a big soul.

Human nature finds it hard to soar to those heights. The treasure is indeed in earthen vessels. With unerring instinct the Early Church was soon 'majoring in minors', and the Church has through the centuries gained itself a name for intolerance and prejudice and backwardness that it is still finding hard to shake off. It is undoubtedly a huge stumbling-block that frequently there is so little difference between those who are inside the Christian community and those who stand outside it. Too often are geriatric grudges kept alive for incredible life spans; too often do jealousies sprout, and hostilities among the 'ins' and the 'outs' flourish. Far too frequently do the abominable no-men put the fear of death into the progressives; and when it comes to touchiness, Albert Orsborn summed it up when he said that church leadership was like dealing with centipedes: 'You can't move without treading on someone's toes!' The sharp point of Nietzche's challenge hurts: 'His disciples will have to look more saved if I am to believe in their Saviour.'

But if one looks closer and in greater detail the picture becomes brighter. For, unlikely as it may seem, some of the people who display pettiness of soul also portray some of the great and lovely and beautiful Christlike qualities. That woman from whom bitterness pours as from a tap when the sensitive point is touched gives of herself unstintingly, amazingly, to the care of neglected children. That man with the built-in 'no' is capable of going not only the second, but the third, fourth and fifth mile once his imagination has been fired. Just as there are no people who are wholly bad, so there are no Christians who are wholly negative and small. Most of them are a fascinating and at times exasperating bundle of contradictions, a strange assortment of the heavenly and the earthly, an impossible mixture of the good and the bad. And often it is the very beauty of the total character that makes the blemishes stand out. They are saints in the making.

What Jesus said about the wheat and the tares growing together temporarily applies not only to the world or the Church, but even more so to the individual personality. In a kind of peaceful co-existence of opposites, good and bad qualities seem able to flourish happily side by side within the same nature in a most disconcerting way. Weeding out the tares takes time. There are no instant mass chemical killers available. Sometimes the person can be genuinely unaware of the tares in his field—a point we shall be developing further in the next chapter—or, at the other extreme, hardness of heart may have set in and the person be only too aware of the tares and know that something ought to and could be done about them, and yet wilfully decide that they should stay. But in the instances we have been citing it is more likely that the soul has consciously or unconsciously accepted Satan's subtle suggestion that a few character flaws are the inevitable and irremediable consequence of being human. This is one of the tempter's chief stratagems. Once he has got us to the state where with unseeing and uncaring eyes we gaze benignly upon a character studded with tares he can safely move on in search of other prey.

But were such believers instead to turn their 'eyes upon Jesus and look full in his wonderful face' much of the smallness around would quickly vanish. For it is when we see his breathtaking generosity, tolerance and magnanimity, his kindness, openness and understanding, his eagerness to believe the best, that the unsightliness of our own bad patches, of those ugly tares, begins to stand out. Gazing at him, new longings and a new hope are born within us. We need not be as we are. 'Away with you, Satan!' We can be like Jesus—for the same Spirit which was at work in him is at work in us. We too can be magnanimous as he was.

According to a legend, Jesus drew near to a crowd that was looking at a dead dog which seemed to have been dragged through the dirt—a vile sight.

'Ugh!' said one, stopping his nose, 'it pollutes the air.'

'How long,' said another, 'shall this foul beast offend our sight?'

'Look at his torn hide,' said a third, 'one could not even cut a shoe out of it.'

'And his ears,' said a fourth, 'all draggled and bleeding.'

'No doubt,' said a fifth, 'he has been hanged for thieving.'

Jesus heard them all and, looking down compassionately on the dead creature, said: 'Pearls cannot equal the whiteness of his teeth.' There was a long silence. And then, being ashamed, they bowed their heads before him and went their way.

18

A remarkably good man

WHATEVER their opinions about the identity and mission of the prophet Jesus, the ordinary people of his day would have agreed on one thing: the Man perfectly filled with the Spirit was a remarkably *good* man. It seemed entirely fitting that the rich young ruler should address him as 'Good Master', and it was typical of Jesus that he should deflect the compliment. 'Why do you call me good? No one is good except God alone' (Luke 18:19). But in a man fully indwelt by that good God, is it surprising to find the quality of goodness shining through?

Goodness is hard to define. It is easier to describe a bad man than a good one and yet, though we cannot express it verbally, we recognise goodness when we see it. It is not softness or sentimentality, for if by definition prime ministers, business tycoons and trade union leaders cannot be good then there is something wrong with our basic concept. 'The goodness of the saint is a peculiar goodness,' says William Sangster in *The Pure in Heart.* 'It flames with the numinous. It is goodness which unconsciously proclaims itself. One feels it as an aura around its possessor. It is incandescent. Its radiations are so powerful that it may be doubted whether anyone could be near it and quite unaware of it. The saint is unconscious of it himself. Blissfully unaware of the impression he makes, he moves on his way *reminding people of Jesus Christ.'*

A Danish missionary officer tells of an incident that moved him deeply. It occurred some months after he arrived as a young officer to try to proclaim the gospel and establish The Salvation Army in a distant part of Celebes. Not knowing the language he felt the only course open to him was to seek to *live* the gospel among the people. He built himself a hut and began to integrate himself into the life of the village. He tilled the fields with the villagers, he hunted with them, he cleared the jungle with them, he ate with them, and as he began to grasp the essentials of their language he tried to tell them about the God of love he served. He had no idea how much, if anything, of his message was reaching them until one afternoon when a villager and he were returning together from a forest clearance. The captain sensed that the young man had something on his mind, and after a while the question came haltingly. 'Tell me,' he said, searching for the right words, 'this God of yours . . . *is he as good as you?'* The message had got through.

But goodness is not only difficult to define, it is hard to acquire. It is only when most of the tares have been weeded out that the quality can be said to begin to appear. It is the fruit that ripens most slowly. It is even possible to receive a powerful baptism of the Spirit which leaves the personality glittering with gifts of the Spirit—and yet be lacking in goodness; the kind of situation that made Paul exclaim: 'I may speak in tongues of men or of angels, but if I am without love, I am a sounding gong or a clanging cymbal' (1 Corinthians 13:1). This strange cleavage which sometimes occurs between the so-called gifts and fruit of the Spirit is a great mystery, and yet it is a fact of experience that touches us in our everyday life.

Extreme cases sometimes help us to see a point more clearly. The Russian monk Rasputin of the time of the Tsars was powerfully gifted spiritually and widely venerated as a holy man, and yet his name was synonymous with intrigue, double-dealing and sheer evil. Or to take a less extreme case, that world evangelist whose spiritual power is such that he sees hundreds of converts at his mammoth rallies, but whose private life leaves much to be desired, is not entirely a character of novels or television dramas. Such people have existed. Or, to take a case from nearer home, it has been known for someone to be baptised in the Spirit and for his spiritual life to be lifted to undreamt-of-heights—and yet for him to remain as self-centred as before. It is also possible to experience the Spirit powerfully on conversion or through a subsequent infilling and yet remain strangely indiscriminating between right and wrong.

Consider this actual case. The new convert at the corps was positively glowing with goodwill, and noticing the run-down condition of the hall offered to paint it in his spare time. The corps officer gratefully accepted, and that evening the new convert arrived complete with a tin of paint and got to work. The captain had expected to provide the paint but each evening his friend arrived with a fresh supply. 'You must let us buy the paint,' remonstrated the captain, not wanting to take advantage of this heart-warming evidence of first love, but the convert would hear of no such thing. But in the end, when the value of the paint supplied seemed far in excess of what could reasonably be expected of a working man, however generous, the captain insisted.

'But you don't understand, captain,' said the convert. 'I work in a factory where they have so much spare paint that it simply stands around. Far better for it to be used for the glory of God. So I've been bringing a tin home with me every day for weeks!'

Paul had to wrestle with this point. His converts were filled with a sense of supernatural power. They gloried in it. But Paul had to try to show them that such power divorced from the qualities of life that Jesus had displayed was meaningless. The force of his words is sometimes lost on us brought up in a tradition which equates religious experience with ethical conduct. For example, he has to say *to the Christians* at Colossae: 'But now you must yourselves lay aside all anger, passion, malice, cursing, filthy talk—have done with them! Stop lying to one another, now that you have discarded the old nature with its deeds and have put on the new nature' (Colossians 3:8, 9). Or, as he might have put it, now that you are Christians stop stealing paint!

But how can it be that sons of God, born of his Spirit, can be so ethically unaware? Parables have a way of illumining truth, and I am indebted to that great teacher, Colonel Gordon Mitchell, for this one:

> Once upon a time a band of robbers descended on the royal palace and stole the king's own baby son, the heir to the throne. He was brought up among them in the forest as one of them, and learnt to steal, to swear and to fight. But one day the king's soldiers ambushed the band and he was taken prisoner. There was something about his bearing that impressed them, however, and the discovery of a birthmark confirmed their hopes: this was indeed the son of the king, the lost heir to the throne. In triumph he was returned to the palace and introduced to his father. He was dressed in the finest robes, seated at a sumptuous meal and told that everything in the kingdom was his. He was the son of the king.
>
> But there was a problem. He had never sat at a table before, he could not speak without cursing, he could not read or write, and knew nothing about governing a kingdom. He might be the son of the king and share all his powers—but from that day onwards *he had to learn to act like a son of a king,* and that was a process that took a long, long time.

Goodness is not gained by some once-and-for-all stroke of omnipotence. It is the result of gradual weeding out of tares and growth in discrimination and Christlike qualities.

19

A remarkably self-controlled man

WHEN the Man perfectly filled with the Spirit 'found in the temple the dealers in cattle, sheep, and pigeons, and the money-changers seated at their tables' he made a whip of cords and drove them out of the temple, sheep, cattle and all. He upset the tables of the money-changers, scattering their coins. 'Then he turned on the dealers in pigeons: "Take them out," he said; "you must not turn my Father's house into a market"' (John 2:14-16). If that seems a strange choice of scene to illustrate the remarkable self-control of Jesus, it is only because self-control is often mistakenly confused with the suppression of our instinctive and emotional drives and responses. Self-control is not the *suppression* but the *harnessing* of them. Jesus did not lose his temper and let fly in all directions when he saw what was going on in the Temple. He used his God-given capacity for anger for God's purposes. But he was in control all the time. The flip-side, as it were, of his fierce passionate love for God and man was a corresponding capacity for wrath which could denounce evil in terrible terms.

A busy executive was once rebuked by a young minister for losing his temper, and he replied: 'Young man, I control more temper every 15 minutes than you will in a lifetime.' Our Lord's capacity for anger exceeded that of any executive but it was harnessed, channelled, directed indignation and was never used selfishly. 'When he was abused he did not retort with abuse, when he suffered he uttered no threats' (1 Peter 2:23).

Had Jesus lived in this century the white heat of his anger would have blazed at the injustices of a world which allows two-thirds of the population to remain undernourished while the other third burns its surpluses. He would have denounced exploitation of the weak by the strong in terms so scathing that he would quickly have been rejected by the establishment. The trouble with his followers today is not that they get angry, it is that they do not get angry enough—and that when they do it is often over small personal issues. Confessed George Matheson: 'There are times when I do well to be angry, but I have mistaken the times!'

This harnessing of all the natural drive, this mastery, discipline and directing of all the forces of the personality toward positive ends, is what Paul termed self-control in his list of the fruit of the Spirit. The word is useful for taking us a step further in our study of how these Christlike qualities can become ours. We have already noted that it is when we look upon Jesus that our faults become revealed. We must now note that just as there can be no *self*-control without the self being engaged, so none of the Christlike qualities of character can be acquired without the active participation of the personality. Christlikeness does not get sprayed on, nor does it just happen to grow while our attention is engaged elsewhere. It is through a process of active co-operation between the Holy Spirit and the self that we become like Christ.

There can be no achievement without effort. This holds good for all realms, including that of sanctification. And Paul underscores in a key passage that whereas 'it is God, who . . . brings to effect in us both the initial willing and the effective action' (a comforting word for those whose sin is the sin of not wanting to advance spiritually) it is our responsibility to 'carry to its perfect conclusion the work of (your) own salvation with fear and trembling' (Philippians 2:12, 13, Barclay, *The Daily Study Bible*). 'Nowhere in the New Testament is the work of salvation more succinctly and epigrammatically stated,' comments William Barclay on these verses.

This does not mean 'sanctification by works'. Because of the former excesses of the Church in stressing 'salvation by works', and the violent swing of the pendulum in Luther's reformation, the Protestant tradition has been fearful of giving the self much if any place in the development of Christian graces. If salvation is by faith, it is argued, sanctification is as well. But there is a big difference. Salvation is primarily change of relationship. By God's unmerited favour I am restored from the forest to the palace, am given a Robe and become the King's own son. It is all of God. I simply accept his favour 'by faith'. But in the long process of learning to act like the son of a King my active participation, not only in faith but also in obedience and effort, becomes indispensable.

This effort on my part does not mean having to embrace an extreme, ascetic 'world-denying' approach to life—a rejection of God's world and of my own nature—though there will be times when the seeker after fullness will seem to reject the good as well as the bad. But if so it is only that he might reach out for the best. Knowing that 'only empty hands can grasp a full God' he empties them even of that which is good, like a child who leaves aside his comic to reach for a book, or a teenager who puts down the pop record to try a light classic, in order to grasp the pearl of greatest price. And when he puts down the penny to pick up the pound it is not because he is forced to do so. It is because he *wants* to do it. It is the natural and spontaneous response of a maturing spirit to a generous God.

In what does effort in spiritual growth consist? The writer to the Hebrews gives us the answer with his picture of the spiritual athlete: 'We must throw off every encumbrance, every sin to which we cling, and run with resolution the race for which we are entered, our eyes fixed on Jesus, on whom faith depends from start to finish' (Hebrews 12:1, 2). With the help of the Spirit, we put our will, with resolution, behind everything that will make us better Christians, and with equal determination throw off or resist anything that will bind us. The spiritual athlete will therefore discipline his body and mind. He will shy away from over-indulgence in any form. He will deliberately avoid exposing himself to situations that could inflame any latent covetousness, greed, envy, base ambition, or lust. Particularly on the latter point ~~with~~ will the Spirit-filled man be careful, remembering Logan Pearsall Smith's warning 'that nature, in one of her grossest economies, has placed the seats of spiritual and amorous rapture so close to each other that one of them is very likely to arouse the other'. He will go out of his way to show love to his enemies. He will actively seek to combat his natural inclination towards selfishness by persevering thoughtfulness and service towards others. He will resist the tendency for the mind to shrink to a narrow introverted circle of interests by opening himself to new knowledge, new ideas, a wider world. He will search the Scriptures and other Christian literature to deepen his faith. He will worship with his brothers and he will pray.

If this were simply yet another programme of self-improvement it would be doomed to defeat. But it is not. The special secret lies in the words of Paul already quoted: 'It is God who brings to effect in us both the initial willing and the effective action.' Herein lies the key. Self-control, and all other Christlike qualities, are 'brought to effect' within us by the Spirit. When we are prepared to co-operate.

As Augustine put it in his inimitable style: 'Without God we cannot—without us God will not.'

20

A remarkably God-aware man

SENSITIVE souls sometimes experience moments of awareness, moments when for an instant their inner eyes are opened and they see the world suffused by divinity. For a brief second they experience eternity. And as they perceive God actively and lovingly at work within his creation, their faith soars, their doubts and fears vanish, their ambitions and values are transmuted, and they long with their whole being to be at one with him. The world with all its seeming contradictions is seen to make wonderful sense. Everything has meaning, everything fits in, and all, all is well, and utterly satisfying. And then the window shuts. But the memory lingers on hauntingly.

Whereas for us these are but very occasional and fleeting glimpses of reality, Jesus, the Man perfectly filled with the Spirit, seems to have had a much more constant awareness of the other dimension. The window was always open to God. He sensed the divine power at work through him, and when he spoke or acted he did so against the backdrop of eternity. Jesus was vividly aware, for example, of the tremendous spiritual resources available to mankind, and saw his own healing powers as an invasion of eternity into the now, and an expression of God's loving concern for his children. It was a deep disappointment to him that so few seemed to share this insight. In Nazareth, 'he was taken aback by their want of faith'. It frustrated him. 'He could work no miracle there' (Mark 6:5, 6). It pained him. 'What an unbelieving and perverse generation! How long shall I be with you? How long must I endure you?' (Mark 9:19).

We sense a similar reaction in the incident when 'he was approached by a leper, who knelt before him begging his help. "If only you will," said the man, "you can cleanse me.".' The phrasing of the request seems to have disturbed Jesus. If only you will . . . with its implied suggestion that he might withhold the blessing being sought. How did Jesus react? Most of the ancient manuscripts of the gospels record that he 'was moved with compassion', but a few of the very old Greek versions of Mark give us a different reading. They tell us that Jesus 'was moved with anger' by the form of the question. 'In warm indignation', translates the *New English Bible,* 'Jesus stretched out his hand, touched him, and said, "Indeed I will; be clean again"' (Mark 1:40, 41).

Something of the same exasperation can also be felt in the incident when the disciples are unable to heal a boy convulsed. When Jesus appears the father pleads with him: 'If it is at all possible for you, take pity upon us and help us.' Jesus must have been vexed by the many 'ifs' that were creeping into the requests for his help. 'If only you would,' the leper had said. 'If only you could,' the father was now saying. Exclaimed Jesus: 'If it is possible! Everything is possible to one who has faith' (Mark 9:22, 23).

But the Man perfectly filled with the Spirit was not only taken aback by the lack of faith shown by his contemporaries in God's active intervention on their behalf. With his insight into the eternal realities of the Kingdom, the trust men place in the passing things of this world struck him as incredible folly. J. B. Phillips tells of some fieldmice living in a cornfield and for whom the solidity and permanence of their field is thc unshakeable reality of their existence. But one day along comes the harvesting machine and in seconds their whole world crumbles and is gone. With our greater knowledge we can see the foolishness of the assumptions made by the mice. But to Jesus it was unbelievable that men could blithely assume that their world, their material possessions and earthly ambitions were in any way more permanent than the cornfield. 'You fool,' he makes God say in the parable to the man who wanted to build bigger barns, 'this very night you must surrender your life; you have made your money—who will get it now?' (Luke 12:20).

The values of the world would make sense if this were the only dimension—but when viewed against the eternal dimension they are shown up for the nonsense they really are. That the spiritual dimension was the ultimate reality was crystal clear to Jesus. He not only taught it, he lived it. William Temple likens the world to a shop-window where thieves have broken in and have changed all the price tags, so that what is truly valuable is marked as cheap, and what is of little worth is shown as being of great value. Through his teaching the Man perfectly filled with the Spirit sought to open men's eyes to the true values of life. But he did more. He himself dared to live with reversed values. The world thought him mad. In the end it killed him.

Those of his followers who have shared his insight and have had the courage to live by it have often been misunderstood. 'If one wrote an account of the "folly" of the saints,' comments William Sangster, 'it would take many volumes. Yet it is, of course, *the plain sense of things* as the saints see life. Looked at in the light of eternity, what madness fortune-building is. How insane that men should scheme for a title which means little enough now, and nothing hereafter! What delusion of the devil leads people to put much store on "things"? What is praise, power or position with the hearse at the door? The saint is distinctive only because he sensibly acts on what he sees. If anybody is a fool, it is not he.'

The cross seemed foolishness to man. But, however contradictory it might sound to human ears, to lose one's life in order to find it has a divine logic all of its own—in the context of eternity. For 'what will a man gain by winning the whole world, at the cost of his true self?' (Luke 9:25).

The Man perfectly filled with the Spirit saw things as God sees them and dared to live by that revelation to the very end.

21

A remarkably world-aware man

THE trouble with some people who have been granted a vision of eternity is that they sometimes find it difficult to keep their feet planted on earth. They become other-worldly. They see this life as merely a preparation for the next. They lose interest in the affairs of this world and withdraw themselves from involvement. After all, are not the things of earth just fleeting shadows and transient dreams? But spiritual experience which does not translate itself into an active and outgoing concern for others and the betterment of the present world is to be suspected. The spiritual life is not, in Evelyn Underhill's graphic phrase, 'a mere cultivation of one's own soul: poking about our interior premises with an electric torch', it is the opening of oneself to the one who is actively at work establishing his Kingdom—the Kingdom in which his will is to be done on earth in the way it is in Heaven.

The Man perfectly filled with the Spirit, whose personal experiencing of that Spirit must have surpassed anything we can imagine, was surprisingly down to earth in his valuation of spiritual experience. He who must often have been, in Paul's phrase, lifted to the third heaven, and have 'exulted in the Holy Spirit' (Luke 10:21) took a pragmatic approach to these things and made it clear that claims to divine encounters have to be validated by their results. 'Beware of false prophets . . .' he said to hearers well-accustomed to vividly-told tales of religious experience. 'You will recognise them by the fruits they bear. Can grapes be picked from briars, or figs from thistles? In the same way, a good tree always yields good fruit, and a poor tree bad fruit. . . . That is why I say you will recognise them by their fruits' (Matthew 7:15-20). It is as if he was saying: 'Do not take a testimony to great spiritual experience at face value. Watch the attitude and conduct of the testifier, and you will know whether his claims are genuine. For it is by the outward results that inner spiritual experience is measured.'

In fact, when one reads the four gospels there is great reticence about spiritual experience as such and little about its cultivation. Even in the Holy Spirit references in John's gospel the accent is on enabling service. Unlike many a guru past and present, the Man perfectly filled with the Spirit did not seek for himself, or preach to others, transcendental states of the mind or supernatural glimpses of glory. He was almost disconcertingly practical and 'this-worldly' in his approach. The Kingdom had to be established—here and now—and he was hard at work in order to make it a reality. Through his experience of the Spirit the vision had become clear and, with it, the power to accomplish. Through times of prayer the vision was maintained and the power channel kept clear. There was a task to be accomplished—and so he preached, and healed and taught and toiled as if haunted by his own words: 'While daylight lasts we must carry on the work of him who sent me; night comes, when no one can work' (John 9:4).

The Christian experience of the Holy Spirit can never be the pursuit of spiritual experience for its own sake, a cultivation of warm, reassuring, comforting feelings. Even to think of the Holy Spirit as a 'comforter' can be misleading, for the English word used in the *Authorised Version* has lost its original force of 'one who makes us brave'. The *parakletos* of whom Jesus spoke is 'the one who enables us to cope' with all the demands and challenges of the created order, and his presence in our lives is invariably a call to action. The outward results of the inner experience of the Spirit that can be legitimately looked for, go far beyond the development of ethical goodness and the various other character traits we have been considering in previous chapters.

The true measure of a man's sanctity cannot be obtained by examining him in isolation. It is in his inter-action with the world and in his handling of its day-to-day activity that the true measure of the man is seen. This even goes beyond what we salvationists commonly term our 'service'. There is an unconscious tendency within us to divide the sacred from the secular, and to consider our service to God as beginning when we come home from earning our daily bread and don our uniform and go down to the hall.

But life cannot be compartmentalised in that way. Sacred and secular are all of a piece—for all things are of God. The divisions exist only in our minds and can mislead us badly. However valuable our Salvation Army 'service' is to God and mankind, it is but a part, and generally speaking a proportionally small part, of the 'service' that we render to God through our total lives. Any concept of the Spirit-filled life which reduces it only to growth in personal holiness and effectiveness in consciously Christian service is inadequate. Unless our experience of the Spirit permeates that which occupies our minds and hands for the greater part of our existence, something is badly wrong. And it is precisely at this point that the greatest challenge comes to anyone seeking to live the life of the Spirit.

When, within a few months of each other, John Boyd received a knighthood and the Order of the Founder, it was as if his nation and his church were jointly recognising his outstanding achievement as a 'militant moderate', a Christian leader of one of the largest trade unions in Britain. Who could possibly begin to measure the tensions and conflicting pressures that Sir John would have experienced as he sought to work out in the tumultuous world of trade unionism what the Spirit had worked in?

Some of the pressures may even have come from fellow salvationists not always understanding of his absences from the corps when his other duties called. But who, when faced with complex management-union pay award negotiations, involving factors such as decimal percentage points of productivity, estimates and projects, index linking, bonuses, holidays, automation, quality control, tea breaks, suspicious management and a union negotiating team reflecting a multitude of shades of opinions—who could possibly know what Jesus would have done under those circumstances? And yet the committed Christian cannot shrink from applying the very best of his intellect and experience and get right in there where it matters if his experience of the Spirit is to mean anything.

Or take Dag Hammarskjöld, that outstanding Secretary-General of the United Nations, whose deep inner life in the Spirit was the spring from which a life of great energy flowed. Dealing with world crises on the grand scale, operating such levers of power as were available to him, involved him in unceasing activity—writing, speaking, phoning, cabling, persuading, cajoling, settling, pushing, arguing, insisting, standing up against, yielding gracefully, coming back again—in order to keep the nations of the world from war. No luxury for him of living on the mountain top surveying from afar the activities below. No, there were arguments to be marshalled and, metaphorically, arms to be twisted and heads to be knocked together. Dag Hammarskjöld knew that his inner knowledge of the Spirit had to be expressed in the affairs of men if it was to have any meaning and that this was the only path to true holiness. He lived what he believed.

Not all are called to be general secretaries of world forums or national unions. But our experience of the Spirit will be judged not so much by our spoken testimony, nor by what we are or do when 'at the corps'. It is by our ability to live out and apply the heavenly vision to the hurly-burly of everyday life that ultimately we will be judged.

22

A remarkably Spirit-gifted man (1)

WHEN John the Baptist sent two of his disciples to ask the Man perfectly filled with the Spirit whether he really was God's chosen one: 'There and then', Luke tells us, 'he cured many sufferers from diseases, plagues, and evil spirits; and on many blind people he bestowed sight. . . . "Go," said Jesus, "and tell John what you have seen and heard: how the blind recover their sight, the lame walk, the lepers are made clean, the deaf hear, the dead are raised to life, the poor are hearing the good news"' (Luke 7:21-23). It was through such 'miracles, portents, and signs' (Acts 2:22) that Jesus was chiefly known, and he himself saw in these powers not only evidence that the Spirit of God was at work through him but also that the new age had dawned. 'If it is by the Spirit of God that I drive out the devils,' he stated after healing a man possessed, 'then be sure the kingdom of God has already come upon you' (Matthew 12:28).

If mighty works and spiritual powers were such a prominent feature of the life and ministry of the Man *perfectly* filled with the Spirit, it is only right that we inquire what part they ought to play in the lives and service of his followers today. The release of hitherto latent spiritual faculties and powers is undoubtedly part of the Holy Spirit's work in and through man. 'In truth, in very truth I tell you,' said Jesus in some of his most tantalising words, 'he who has faith in me will do what I am doing; and he will do greater things still because I am going to the Father' (John 14:12).

Paul speaks of powers released in the believer as *gifts* of the Spirit. This gives us a useful tool for analysing the work of the Spirit, though it would probably be misleading to draw too distinctive boundary lines between the various gifts or to take Paul's lists as in any way exhaustive. In the same way as the talents of a multi-talented person are not so much separate gifts as aspects of a total personality, so the gifts of the Spirit shade into one another like the colours of the spectrum and what matters supremely is the light of the Spirit's work as a whole. Among the gifts of the Spirit which Paul lists and which we see operative in the life of the Man perfectly filled with the Spirit is the gift of 'mighty works', the working of miracles. The early Christians felt that something of the same power that enabled Jesus to calm a storm, walk on water, and feed 5,000 men, was in evidence wherever the Spirit was at work. 'When God gives you the Spirit and works miracles among you . . .' comments Paul (Galatians 3:5), taking the causal link for granted.

The New Testament, Church history and the testimonies of those powerfully indwelt by the Spirit provide plentiful illustrations of the occurrence of seemingly supernatural interventions, answers to prayer, cases of supernatural guidance and miracles—major and minor—wherever the Spirit has been released. It is not easy to explain these phenomena, and perhaps the nearest one can get to a rational account of these seeming breaks in the natural chain of cause and effect, is that it is the present incompleteness of our knowledge that makes them seem supernatural and therefore miraculous. As a primitive man emerging from a jungle and faced with a television set would conclude it to be supernatural and miraculous because of his lack of knowledge, so we call miraculous those factors which as yet are outside our realm of understanding. In some way not yet understood, he who is filled with the Spirit has an increased sensitivity to the resources of the spiritual dimension. We cannot explain the operation of these 'higher laws' but that 'coincidences begin to happen' when the Spirit indwells a man has been the experience of the Church throughout the ages.

When it comes to the gift of healing, which Paul also includes in his list, commentary becomes easier because the purpose of the gift is more readily evident, but we still have to admit that our knowledge of how these powers operate is extremely limited. The gift was powerfully operative in the Man perfectly filled with the Spirit. The many instances of healing are too well known to need mention here, but it is important to note that they covered many different diseases, some of them well beyond the range of psychosomatic conditions.

Jesus also believed that he cast out demons by the power of God. He felt, as James D. G. Dunn puts it in *Jesus and the Spirit,* 'the power of God flowing through him to overcome other superhuman power, evil power, to restore and make whole. When he spoke or stretched out his hand something happened—the sufferer was relieved, the prisoner freed, the evil departed.' We are too far from the events to know how the various cases would be diagnosed in the light of modern knowledge, but the fact remains that Jesus was able to heal mental suffering.

Again, the witness of the New Testament, Church history and contemporary experience would confirm that healing powers have been released through the Spirit within some believers, and that the sick have been healed in response to faith and prayer. 'This is in perfect harmony with the views and experience of The Salvation Army from the beginning,' wrote William Booth. 'Nothing to the contrary has ever been taught by our authority, and numerous instances of faith healing have occurred in the Army throughout its history.'

It is something of a tragedy that extravagances have gathered round the subject of spiritual healing, and that for many it has become associated with spectacular events in crowded stadiums under the glare of television lights. Spiritual healing is rarely spectacular and instant. Mostly it is a gradual response of the diseased organism to the persistent, costly prayer and faith of the one through whom the healing powers are being mediated, whether that mediation be direct to a sick person physically present, or to someone far distant.

There is, of course, extensive literature on the subject, and it is to be hoped that with the general advance of scientific knowledge our understanding of the possibilities and also the limitations of drawing upon these sources of healing energy around us will increase. But however inadequate our theoretical knowledge, the central fact remains. The healing powers mediated by the Man perfectly filled with the Spirit are being released in some of his followers today.

23

A remarkably Spirit-gifted man (2)

WHEN we consider the ministry of the Man perfectly filled with the Spirit as prophet, teacher and counsellor, we see operative a whole cluster of gifts of the Spirit listed by Paul. We have already noted the spiritual authority which emanated from him, and we must now look at the quality of Spirit-empowered speaking which characterised his utterances to groups and individuals. Jesus was not only a supremely talented, imaginative, creative and eloquent speaker, his words conveyed a spiritual power which compelled attention and convinced his hearers.

Paul speaks of the gift of 'wise speech' and the ability to 'put the deepest knowledge into words' (1 Corinthians 12:8). He also has much to say about the gift of prophecy. Prophecy in this setting carries the sense of forth-telling, not fore-telling. The *New English Bible* translates it 'inspired utterance' (Romans 12:6). It is virtually an exhortation, address or sermon. Regarding such words of exhortation, Paul comments that they have 'power to build; they stimulate and they encourage' (1 Corinthians 14:3), and that when a visitor enters the church he will hear 'something that searches his conscience and brings conviction, and the secrets of his heart are laid bare. So he will fall down and worship God, crying, "God is certainly among you!"' (1 Corinthians 14:24, 25). Inspired utterance; wise words that express the deepest knowledge, that build, stimulate, encourage; that search the conscience, bring conviction, lay bare the secrets of the heart, and cause the hearer to fall down and worship God—could a better description be found of the impact the Lord's words made on his hearers? And the picture is completed when one adds to the above the gift of spiritual insight which Jesus also possessed to a remarkable degree. Though Paul does not specifically name it as a gift, it would be close in the spectrum to the gift of discernment which he mentions.

Through intuitive insight Jesus could read the hearts of men and diagnose their condition. This enabled him to get right to the heart of the matter—as with Nicodemus and the Samaritan woman—and to speak the word of help and healing. That this was a power commonly ascribed to men of God is revealed by the Pharisee's slighting remark when he saw the woman anointing Jesus' feet with myrrh: 'If this fellow were a real prophet, he would know who this woman is that touches him, and what sort of woman she is, a sinner' (Luke 7:39). But, in fact, in Jesus this faculty of spiritual insight was so heightened that it led John to comment: 'He knew men so well, all of them, that he needed no evidence from others about a man, for he himself could tell what was in a man' (John 2:25).

That these powers were operative in the Early Church hardly needs commenting. It would be impossible to account for the impact of Peter's words on the day of Pentecost without postulating such an 'x' factor. And Paul's declaration to the Corinthians is instructive: 'The word I spoke, the gospel I proclaimed, did not sway you with subtle arguments; it carried conviction by spiritual power, so that your faith might be built not upon human wisdom but upon the power of God' (1 Corinthians 2:4, 5).

Similarly God's servants throughout the history of the Church have frequently found their words invested with spiritual power, and in challenging moments have discovered the truth of the words of Jesus: 'do not begin worrying about . . . what you will say. For when the time comes the Holy Spirit will instruct you what to say' (Luke 12:11, 12). Has not every sensitive preacher felt at some time the Holy Spirit using his words to 'confute the world, and show where wrong and right and judgement lie'? (John 16:8). The rapid expansion of The Salvation Army in its early days, when untutored young men and women were used by God for the conversion of thousands, can only be explained in these terms.

Charles Finney became exceptionally powerful in his speaking following an infilling of the Spirit. 'I immediately', he recalls, 'found myself endued with such power from on high that a few words dropped here and there to individuals were the means of their immediate conversion. My words seemed to fasten like barbed arrows on the souls of men. They cut like a sword. They broke the heart like a hammer.'

In looking back over his ministry, Finney wrote: 'Sometimes I would find myself in a great measure empty of this power. I would go out and visit, and find that I made no saving impression. I would then set apart a day for private fasting and praying, fearing that this power had departed from me, and would inquire anxiously after the reason for this apparent emptiness. After humbling myself, and crying out for help, the power would return upon me with all its freshness. This has been the experience of my life.'

How should we look upon these various powers that can be released through the indwelling of the Spirit? Paul is clear on the matter. 'About gifts of the Spirit,' he says, 'there are some things of which I do not wish you to remain ignorant' (1 Corinthians 12:1). The first point he makes is that God gives different gifts to different people—but they all spring from the same Spirit. 'There are varieties of service, but the same Lord. There are many forms of work, but all of them, in all men, are the work of the same God' (1 Corinthians 12:4-6).

The second point is a consequence of the first, that each of us will therefore have a gift, or a span of gifts, which is to be, as it were, our God-given forte in Christian service. 'In each of us', he says, 'the Spirit is manifested in one particular way, for some useful purpose' (1 Corinthians 12:7).

This insight should not be limited to the list of gifts which follows in that particular chapter, for in other writings Paul extends the list of gifts. To the Romans, for example, he writes: 'The gifts we possess differ as they are allotted to us by God's grace, and must be exercised accordingly: the gift of inspired utterance, for example, in proportion to a man's faith; or the gift of administration, in administration. A teacher should employ his gift in teaching, and one who has the gift of stirring speech should use it to stir his hearers. If you give to charity, give with all your heart; if you are a leader, exert yourself to lead; if you are helping others in distress, do it cheerfully' (Romans 12:6-8). 1 Corinthians 12:28 extends the list further.

The third point Paul makes, in 1 Corinthians 12:14-26, is that all gifts are equally needful. All form part of the body of Christ, and no part of the body can therefore say to another, 'I do not need you.'

But, fourthly, in the famous 13th chapter and the beginning of the next, he makes the point that gifts exercised without love are ultimately meaningless, and that we must therefore 'put love first' —and Spirit-empowered exhortation next (1 Corinthians 14:1).

Few believers will find themselves gifted with such a wide span of gifts as the man perfectly gifted by the Spirit, and none will experience the unique fullness of those powers that were his. But every one of us has the divine duty and privilege to seek the release within us of those gifts which the Spirit, who distributes 'separately to each individual at will' (1 Corinthians 12:11), has granted us. And gifts are granted to be used—and to be developed in the service of Christ.

24

A remarkably integrated man

THE winsomeness, fascination and uniqueness of the character of the man perfectly filled with the Spirit lies largely in the poise in which he managed to hold opposing virtues. His personality was an amazing balance of contrasting qualities. We noted this point when contrasting the stern authority which emanated from him with the more tender and warm qualities which made him such an attractive figure. But the point has recurred. He who was so utterly uncompromising with sin was tenderness itself when dealing with a sinner. He who personified energy, drive and activity had a serenity of heart beyond human understanding. He who gave himself in an outflowing of spiritual power knew how to be constantly open to the inpouring of spiritual resources. He who gave his heart to God gave his hand to man. The fearless one was also gentle. He who radiated joy knew suffering. The man who could proclaim 'but *I* say unto you' could also take the bowl of water and wash his disciples' feet.

We say of someone who manages to combine in a harmonious whole the contrasting elements of his personality that he is a well integrated person. In those terms, Jesus was a remarkably well integrated man. He had found the secret of fusing together seeming opposites, and thus creating beauty and effectiveness. But this balancing of opposing virtues, which could be said to be the key element in the character of Jesus, is something the human personality finds difficult to achieve. Dr Bushnell expresses our predicament well: 'Men undertake to be spiritual, and they become ascetic; or endeavouring to hold a liberal view of the comforts and pleasure of society, they are soon buried in the world, and slaves to its fashion; or, holding scrupulous watch to keep out every particular sin, they become legal and fall out of liberty; or charmed with the noble and heavenly liberty, they run to negligence and irresponsible living; so the earnest become violent, the fervent fanatical and censorious, the gentle waver, the firm turn bigots, the liberal grow lax, the benevolent ostentatious.'

'Poor human infirmity can hold nothing steady,' he concludes. But it is just in this that the very key to Christlike living lies. The balance must somehow be attained. Emphasising certain key virtues is not the answer, for integration which is achieved by the suppression of contrasting qualities leaves the personality crippled and unwholesome. The personality therefore finds itself trying to maintain a creative tension, but more often than not it seems like being in the middle of a tug of war—not between virtue and vice, but between opposing virtues.

However, it is not only opposing virtues of character that have to be held in tension. A balance must also be achieved between the demands of the many and varied roles we are called upon to play in life, however virtuous and praiseworthy each might be in itself. The problem with many of us is, as Thomas R. Kelly explains, that: 'We are trying to be several selves at once, without all our selves being organised by a single mastering life within us. Each of us tends to be not a single self, but a whole committee of selves. There is the civic self, the professional self, the literary self.

'And each of our selves is in turn a rank individualist, not co-operative but shouting out his vote loudly for himself when the voting time comes. And all too commonly we follow the common method of getting a quick decision among conflicting claims within us. It is as if we had a chairman of our committee of the many selves within us, who does not integrate the many into one but who merely counts the votes at each decision, and leaves the disgruntled minorities.

'The claims of each self are still pressed. If we accept service on a committee on education, we still regret we can't help with a Sunday-school class. We are not integrated. We are distraught. We feel honestly the pull of many obligations and try to fulfil them all, and we are therefore unhappy, uneasy, strained, oppressed and fearful that we shall be shallow.'

Paul's cry for help echoes our own: 'Miserable creature that I am, who is there to rescue me out of this body doomed to death?' But the reassuring answer comes at once: 'God alone, through Jesus Christ our Lord!' (Romans 7:24, 25). For there is a way through, a way leading to what Thomas Kelly describes as an 'amazing equilibrium of life, an amazing effectiveness of living', in which 'the fretful calls of life are integrated, where no as well as yes can be said with confidence. Such lives, integrated, unworried by the tangles of close decisions, unhurried, cheery, fresh, positive, are not the lives of people of dallying idleness nor of obviously mooning meditation; they are people busy carrying their full load as well as we, with quiet joy and springing step. They are poised and at peace.'

The way through is to become utterly attentive and utterly obedient to that still small voice which speaks to us in the centre of our being—the voice of God who indwells us. Utter attention and utter obedience means resolving to surrender all else and even, if necessary, order our outward affairs so as to be at every moment attentive and open to him. It may sound demanding but it is the divine way through to that integration, that amazing equilibrium and effectiveness of living, which the human heart longs for.

But what about the achievement of a balanced, Christlike *character* in which every virtue is balanced by its contrasting virtue? The way through is similar. We attend utterly and we obey implicitly the whispers of the Spirit within—none other than the 'Spirit of Christ' (Romans 8:9)—and with the eyes of our understanding we keep watching and studying and learning from the life of Jesus of Nazareth as recorded in the gospels. We seek to co-operate both at conscious and unconscious level with the Spirit.

The qualities of a Christlike life cannot be gained one by one like a scout setting out to get activity badges. It is not a matter of concluding that one has, for example, attained love and joy, and deciding to go in for peace. The sanctifying process, growth in Christlikeness, is a much more subtle and complex development within the personality. But of one thing we can be quite sure: the one who started the good work in us will not leave us unaided, or allow our growth to become distorted. He will guide us, sometimes by speaking directly to us, sometimes by speaking through his word, or through a friend, a book, a sermon, a testimony, or the shining life of a fellow believer. Our task is to remain open to him, to listen—and to co-operate. 'Of one thing I am certain,' said Paul, 'the One who started the good work in you will bring it to completion by the Day of Christ Jesus' (Philippians 1:6). Therein lies the Christian hope.

25

Ourselves—the gift becomes available

THROUGHOUT this book we have noted how the special qualities that characterised Jesus of Nazareth were enhanced by his experience of the Holy Spirit at the River Jordan and how new powers were released within him from that moment. It was when he became 'armed with the power of the Spirit' that his mission began and the full impact of his personality, words and deeds began to be felt.

We need to observe, however, that these qualities and powers did not transfer themselves to his followers during his lifetime. With the exception of the times of the mission, his disciples did not share the special powers of their Master. Indeed, they were perplexed at their inability to heal. Nor did they share the distinctive traits of his character. They were harassed where he was serene, they were small-minded where he was magnanimous, they were ready to compromise where he refused, and when it came to the crunch and he was prepared to die for what he stood for, they all forsook him and fled.

If our Lord's ministry were to be seen as solely a teaching ministry, one would have to conclude that it was largely a failure. But the story does not end with the cross. It continues with the resurrection and the giving of the Spirit. For through the Easter and Pentecost events something of the very qualities and powers which had been Christ's became available to his followers. In Paul van Buren's phrase, they 'became contagious'. What could not be taught, could now be caught. And it was in the giving of the Spirit on the day of Pentecost that the new era began. The Spirit which had indwelt Jesus now indwelt his followers. They shared his secret. They experienced—however partially and imperfectly—what he had experienced in all its perfect fullness.

The effects were immediate and electric. When Peter spoke, his words carried such spiritual power that there were 3,000 converts. The disciples who had been hiding out of fear of the authorities, became irrepressible challengers of those self-same authorities. A spirit of exultant joy pervaded everything and 'many marvels and signs were brought about through the apostles' (Acts 2:43). 'In the end', comments Luke, 'the sick were actually carried out into the streets and laid there on beds and stretchers, so that even the shadow of Peter might fall on one or another as he passed by; and the people from the towns round Jerusalem flocked in, bringing those who were ill or harassed by unclean spirits, and all of them were cured' (Acts 5:15, 16). The sense of love and caring was such that 'Not a man of them claimed any of his possessions as his own, but everything was held in common,' and 'the apostles bore witness with great power to the resurrection of the Lord Jesus' (Acts 4:32, 33), with the result that 'numbers of men and women were added to their ranks as believers' (Acts 5:14).

The disciples also discovered, to their surprise and joy, that this new power which indwelt them was not an impersonal force, but had personality. And, most marvellous of all, had the personality of Jesus, the one they had grown to love and thought they had lost for ever. Jesus was not dead. He had not departed from them. He was alive and he was present—in the Spirit. The early Christians were unversed in the subtleties of trinitarian doctrine. They sensed, they felt, they knew that the Holy Spirit was making Christ real to them and that in the Holy Spirit they were experiencing the risen Christ, and they happily spoke of this great reality in their lives sometimes as Jesus, sometimes as Christ, sometimes as the risen Christ, sometimes as the Spirit, or the Spirit of Christ, or the Spirit of God, or simply as God.

Opening oneself to that reality, receiving the Holy Spirit, is an indispensable element of our initiation as Christians. In the experience of salvation our sins are forgiven, we become members of God's great family, and we are regenerated by the Holy Spirit—we are born again. Though the imagery is different, the idea is basically the same. 'No one', said Jesus, 'can enter the Kingdom of God without being born from water and spirit. Flesh can give birth only to flesh; it is spirit that gives birth to spirit. . . . The wind blows where it wills; you hear the sound of it, but you do not know where it comes from, or where it is going. So with everyone who is born from spirit' (John 3:5, 6, 8). Without the Spirit there can be no Christian, and no Christian can be without the Spirit, for as we noted at the start of this book, 'if a man does not possess the Spirit of Christ, he is no Christian' (Romans 8:9).

Despite the unique situation in which the disciples found themselves living, as it were in the overlap of the ages, it would be fair to say that it was on the day of Pentecost that they were initiated into the Christian experience—that they were born of the Spirit. That this is how it seemed to Peter is confirmed by his choice of words when he later gave an account of the conversion of Cornelius to the church at Jerusalem. 'Hardly had I begun speaking,' he reported, 'when the Holy Spirit came upon them, just as upon us at the beginning. Then I recalled what the Lord had said: "John baptized with water, but you will be baptized with the Holy Spirit." God gave them no less a gift than he gave us when we put our trust in the Lord Jesus Christ' (Acts 11:15-17).

The points we have been considering are of great practical relevance to us in our quest to be like Jesus and to share something of the qualities and powers that were his. For anyone feeling dissatisfied with his inner life, who finds himself hungering and thirsting for greater reality in his spiritual awareness, and who longs to see greater evidence of the Spirit's indwelling in both his character and service, the crucial question will be this: If I already 'possess the Spirit of Christ' in virtue of being a committed Christian, have I then experienced all there is to be experienced, and received all there is to be received?

By no means. Spiritual hunger is part of God's working in our lives. It is his way of making us aware that there are vaster dimensions of spiritual life. If the hunger is there it is because God longs to satisfy us. The way through to these greater dimensions of life for those born of the Spirit will be the subject matter of the last chapter of this book. But this chapter would not be complete without considering another possible explanation for spiritual poverty. It could be that though we have long been associated with the religious life in all its external forms, we have never actually taken the step of repentance and faith that leads us to be born of the Spirit. This must not be confused with a great emotional conversion experience. Relatively few people, especially from a Christian background, are granted such emotionally memorable moments of entry into the Kingdom. Many, in fact, find it difficult to be precise about the moment when it occurred. But he who has put his trust in the Son of God has, as John puts it, 'the witness in himself' (1 John 5:10, *AV*)—some inner confirmation, sooner or later, that he is a child of God.

If this assurance is entirely lacking, the above diagnosis may have to be applied.

26

Ourselves—stirring the gift into flame

WHEN writing to his convert Timothy, Paul uses a phrase which is full of meaning for anyone born of the Spirit who longs to share the qualities of character and spiritual powers of the man perfectly filled with the Spirit. 'Stir into flame,' he writes. 'Stir into flame the gift of God which is within you through the laying on of my hands' (2 Timothy 1:6). Timothy had been born again, he had received the gift of the Spirit. Paul had been present at his conversion and had personally prayed with him. But now Paul ventures to suggest that instead of the experience resulting in a blazing fire giving off heat and light, it had resulted in something more akin to smouldering embers emitting wisps of grey smoke. 'That is why I now remind you', he says, 'to stir into flame the gift of God which is within you.'

It is undoubtedly true that some Christians fail to enter into the fullness of the Christian experience at their moment of initiation to faith. Instead of fire there is smoke. The reasons for this can be many and varied—ranging from a lack of knowledge of what the full Christian experience should include, to a lack of faith or obedience on their part, or even some deep-seated psychological blockage which hinders them from enjoying in experience what in reality is theirs as heirs of God. They enter into an experience which though real fails to satisfy. They remain seekers. The fire has yet to be stirred into flame.

It would also be true to say that many believers who have found themselves in that condition have come alive in Christ—the fire has burst into flame—through a further spiritual experience which remains for ever vivid in their memory by its transforming significance. Such, for example, was the experience of Francis of Assisi and John Wesley. In fact this pattern of experience occurs so frequently that many have felt that it is the classic pattern of Christian experience. Any such further epochal crisis experience is best accounted for doctrinally as a *completion* of our experience of salvation. What has been ours all along now becomes so in actuality. We are like heirs who have suddenly stumbled to the fact that the inheritance is a good deal larger than we had at first thought. But there is really no such thing as a basic pattern of experience. God deals with us individually and the variety of experience is therefore as wide as humanity itself. And in the same way that some would find it difficult to pin-point the moment of initiation into faith, others would find it hard to be precise about a specific moment of completion. For them the Christian experience has seemed more like many moments of revelation, illumination, empowering and blessing—each adding some further insight or increase of spiritual vitality. And such visitations, sought or unsought, cannot be imprisoned within a precise doctrinal framework.

Other believers would have to admit that there have been few 'peak' events in their Christian experience. They probably find themselves uncomfortable with the thought of special moments. To them, the Christian life has seemed more like a gradual unfolding of understanding, a growing openness to things spiritual, an increasing drawing on the resources available, a deepening friendship. For a few others, the Christian walk has possibly seemed to have little or no emotional content. Their walk has been the walk of faith. For not only are there differences in the patterns of experience, there are also differences in our temperamental 'giftedness' or innate capacity for spiritual experience.

An important point needs to be noted here. If in our thinking we restrict the possibility of experiencing God only to spiritual experience, as such—or worse, only to that which appears unusual and irrational within religious experiences—we shall be closing ourselves off from the richness of God's full revelation of himself. We shall be making the mistake, noted in a previous chapter, of wanting to separate the Creator-God from the Saviour-God. Man experiences God supremely through the indwelling of the Holy Spirit but we must not forget that he can also be found in the beauty of nature, in the order of the universe, in the wonders of art, a musical cadence, in the thrill of creativity, the joy of friendship, the gift of love, in the cry of the new-born baby. God is not a God of religion only. He is God of all life—and those that have eyes to see and ears to hear will meet him again and again within his creation.

But having made all these necessary points, it nevertheless remains true that many Christians feel themselves to be living at a substandard level of Christian experience. It is not an occasional passing thought. Intuitively they know that there is more to the full Christian life than they have yet experienced, and they cannot ignore the inner yearnings.

For those who thus feel the inadequacy of their present state, there is a significant point of grammar in the words Paul addressed to Timothy. The text does not say, 'Let the gift of God be stirred into flame'. Neither does it say, 'let God stir the gift into flame'. It is quite clear by the grammar of the sentence that it is Timothy himself who is expected to take action. 'You stir into flame the gift of God.' In other words, there is something that we can and ought to do about our spiritual condition. The initiative lies with us rather than with God.

If this seems contrary to that strong emphasis on 'by grace through faith' within the Protestant tradition, which we have already noted, we need to remind ourselves again of the difference there is between receiving the gift of salvation 'by grace through faith' and its subsequent development in the sanctifying process. It is God that gives us our gifts, both natural and spiritual. They are 'not a reward for work done. There is nothing for anyone to boast of' (Ephesians 2:9). But what we *do* with those gifts depends very much on ourselves. This rule holds as true in the spiritual realm.

How sad if on the great judgment day God has to say to someone, 'I intended you to be another Michelangelo—I gave you the gift, but you did nothing with it.' Or to another, 'I intended you to be another Beethoven—I gave you the gift, but you did nothing with it.' But how infinitely more tragic if he has to say to one of us: 'I meant you to be like my Son Jesus—the man perfectly filled with the Spirit. I gave you the gift—the gift of the Spirit, but you did nothing with it.'

What God requires of us in order that the gift of the Spirit within us might develop into a blazing fire is *increased co-operation* with the work of the Spirit and *increased expectancy.* It is by saying yes to the voice within, and by keeping on saying yes, that our co-operation with the Spirit increases. Our turning away from all that would hinder spiritual progress needs to be specific and thoroughgoing, and, in William Booth's phrase, our consecration needs to keep pace with God's revelation.

We can be quite sure that the Spirit, 'who brings to effect in us both the initial willing and the effective action', will not leave us floundering. The next step to be taken in the co-operative process will be clearly marked and the necessary grace available. Our expectancy will increase in the measure that we deliberately open ourselves to influences that will fuel our faith. It is as we attend to Christ and 'look full in his wonderful face', as we ponder the promises of Scripture and seek out God in prayer, and read and hear the testimonies of those who already have found the secret, that our own hunger and thirst for spiritual completion will be increased, and our vision of its possibility fired.

The key lies in the will. Through the spurring and with the help of the Spirit within we determine to obey and we determine to attend. It is as we attend that faith is born. For faith cannot be achieved by an effort of will. It is the indirect, effortless consequences of a mind and heart deliberately exposed and receptively open to the marvels of God's promises and activity. Through our obedience our faith will increase and as our faith increases so will our capacity for obedience. For co-operation and expectancy cannot be separated. They are as closely linked as the right and left feet of the pilgrim advancing along the path, the forward movement of the one impulsing the progress of the other.

As our consecration and faith deepen until the very roots of our mind and being are touched, so the embers of the fire within will begin to kindle. The first small flame will catch alight, then another, then another—until the whole fire burns with the divine brightness. And in the light of that glow will be seen within us the reflection of the beauty and power of the man from Nazareth—Jesus, the man perfectly filled with the Spirit.

The work of a moment? Possibly. But more likely the work of many moments—the work of a lifetime.

Epilogue

Jesus: John baptised with water, but you, you, not many days from now will be baptised with the Holy Spirit!

Peter: Lord, has the time come?

John: Are you going to restore the kingdom to Israel?

Jesus: It is not for you to know the times or dates . . . but you will receive power, you will receive power when the Holy Spirit comes on you, and *then* . . .

Chorus: (Clamouring) Now! Now, Lord! Now!

Jesus: (Silencing them with upraised hand) Then you will be my witnesses not only in Jerusalem, but throughout Judaea and Samaria and indeed, indeed to the ends of the earth!

Chorus: (Turning as if to go) Jerusalem, Judaea, Samaria, the ends of the earth . . .

Jesus: Wait!

Jesus and chorus:

No need to look so glum, don't leave Jerusalem,
The Spirit's going to come,
Hear what I say, You've got to stay!
We've got to stay!
Don't go away! . . .
And you've got to pray, You've got to pray.
We've got to pray. . . .

* * *

Ask! Ask! Ask! and it shall be given;
Seek! Seek! Seek! and you're sure to find;
Knock! Knock! Knock! and the door will open,
For God! God! God! is so good and kind, O yes,
So ask! Ask! Ask! and it shall be given;
Seek! Seek! Seek! and you're sure to find;
Knock! Knock! Knock! and the door will open,
For God! God! God! is so good and kind.

* * *

Girl: 'And whatever you ask in my name,
You'll have it,' Jesus said;
'The power to teach, the power to preach,
The power to raise the dead!'

Peter: (Rapidly and excitedly) 'Is there a father among you who will offer his son a snake when he asks for a fish, or a scorpion when he asks for an egg? If you, then, bad as you are, know how to give your children what is good for them, how much more will the heavenly Father give the Holy Spirit to those who ask him?'

Chorus: Fire must fall, or we'll be no good,
Fire must fall, if it only would!
Fire must fall, or we'll cut no ice,
Fire must burn ev'ry secret vice!
Fire must burn all the bad in us,
Cauterise what is cancerous! . . .
Fire will give us the pow'r, the plus!
Fall then, fire, *and fall on us!*

* * *

Chorus: Burning, burning, brightly burning,
Brightly burning Fire divine,
Satisfy my spirit's yearning,
Fill this empty soul of mine.

Burning, burning, always burning,
Holy Spirit, stay with me;
To your will my will is turning,
What you will I want to be.

Burning, burning, deeply burning,
Deeply burning holy Fire,
Now, your perfect plan discerning,
Your design is my desire.

Burning, burning, gently burning,
Gently burning Fire within,
From your love my love is learning,
Now I feel your work begin.

* * *

Ambitions clamour to control my mind,
And pleasing prospects I see,
But first and foremost in my heart I find
A nobler purpose for me:

To be like Jesus!
This hope possesses me,
In every thought and deed,
This is my aim, my creed;
To be like Jesus!
This hope possesses me,
His Spirit helping me,
Like him I'll be.

In ev'ry field of life I have high hopes,
And for achievement aspire,
But this ambition holds the highest place,
And burns within me like fire:

Whatever I may lose, I mean to win
Some faint resemblance to Christ...
For this alone I'll work, for this I'll pray,
All other aims sacrifice:

—Selected from *Spirit* (Gowans/Larsson)